# Canadian Country
# Preserves & Wines

# Canadian Country Preserves & Wines

**Blanche Pownall Garrett**

James Lewis & Samuel, Publishers
Toronto/1974

Drawings on pages 32, 37, 39, 48, 54, 55, 56, 62, 63, 65, 70, 91, 106, 110, 118 and 121 from *Guide to Common Edible Plants of British Columbia.* Reprinted with permission of the British Columbia Provincial Museum.

Drawings on pages 36, 74, 75, 87, 113 and 117 from *Plants from Sea to Sea* by F.H. Montgomery. Reprinted by permission of McGraw-Hill Ryerson Limited.

Drawings on pages 42, 68 and 81 from *Native Wild Plants* by F. H. Montgomery. Reprinted by permission of McGraw-Hill Ryerson Limited.

Cloth 0-88862-063-2
Paper 0-88862-066-7

Cover design/Don Fernley

James Lewis & Samuel
35 Britain Street
Toronto

Printed and bound in Canada

*for*
*Rebecca and Stephen,*
*who helped*

# Contents

**Bibliography**

# *Acknowledgements*

To attempt to list by name all those who have helped me would be a more formidable task than the writing of this book. Many of them died long ago, even their names are now forgotten; but they bequeathed to us, in the faded pages of tattered old notebooks, their secrets of this culinary art. I am grateful to the friends, acquaintances, and in some instances, almost total strangers who have placed these treasured documents at my disposal.

To the local botanists, historians and librarians in various Canadian communities who have aided me in my search;

To the many friends who, sharing the hobby, have traded tips and recipes and acted as intrepid tasters:

Thank you.

Blanche Pownall Garrett
Peterborough, Ontario
April 1974

# Foreword

This book is the result of two absorbing interests I have pursued for more than a quarter of a century. One is old recipes. The other is the plants that grow in Canada and their uses, historical as well as modern.

The first Canadian cookbook was printed in Kingston, Ontario, in 1831. But for a century before that, wilderness women were sharing recipes with their similarly isolated neighbours. They also traded seeds, sent or brought from their European homelands and carefully hoarded. Gardens were started even before the stumps had been cleared. And from the native peoples, the Indians, the settlers learned to recognize and make use of the wild plant wealth around them.

In this day of plenty, when many stores, even in small villages, carry a bountiful supply of fruits and fresh vegetables out of season, it is difficult for us to comprehend the importance of plants in the lives of Canadian pioneers. After months of inadequate and monotonous winter fare, how eagerly they must have gathered the wild onions and watercress, the dandelion greens and edible ferns, in the first weeks of each spring. And each autumn, how apprehensive they must have been as heavy frosts put an end to their gardens for another long Canadian winter.

Plants, cultivated and wild, meant survival in a new and unbelievably difficult land. Not only did plants provide food; they were tonic, antiseptic and medicine as well. Doctors were few and far between, so each family had to develop its own treasury of home remedies. When the settlers became convinced that wild rose hips and mountain ash berries gave protection against scurvy, that hawthorn wine was beneficial for heart trouble, that an infusion of dandelion leaves eased kidney infection, they looked about for ways in which such plants might be preserved for winter use. So, a rich anthology of recipes accumulated in each community – for cordials and wines and vinegars, for pickled and preserved fruits, for chutneys and jams and jellies.

Early Canadian cookbooks were much more than recipe collections. Their worn pages reflect a way of life that dealt with each day's problems in the only possible way, by making use of what was at hand. So – along with directions for the making of corn fritters, apple dumplings, pumpkin nut loaf, elderberry gin – we find instructions for making concoctions against the dreaded ague (malarial fever), a liniment for inflamed joints, powerful potions for ailing cows and oxen, and even a method of steeping larkspur seeds, "to expel nameless intruders from children's heads."

History has been known to repeat itself. If today's prices of food and drink continue to soar, it may well be that we who find preserving such a fascinating art will also reap its practical economic advantages. The pleasant pastime of wild plant cookery is one way of helping to live with a food budget that is completely out of control. Meanwhile, I know of no household hobby that gives such pleasure and satisfaction.

B. P. G.

# *How to use this book*

The recipes in this book make use of both culti-vated and wild plants. The plants are listed in alphabetical order, from apple to zucchini. The recipes fit into five basic categories: *beverages; catsups, chutneys and relishes; conserves, mar-malades and preserves; jams and jellies;* and, finally, *pickles.* In order to keep this book down to a reasonable length, I have not included a recipe for each plant in each of these categories. This should not be interpreted to mean that you can't, for example, make bakeapples into conserve as well as into jam. Once the basic method of making a certain preserve or wine is mastered, most plants are fair game.

Before starting any of the recipes, *please read the next few introductory pages.* They will tell you about terms you might not find in a standard dictionary, simple equipment that you will need, general hints that might save you from making unnecessary mistakes, and the basic procedure for making each type of preserve or wine.

The careful reader will also notice that the recipes do not tell you how many jars you will get from this jam or that conserve. Except for wines and jellies (see pp. 20 and 22, respectively), varia-tion in fruit size makes quantity almost impossible to predict; but since I generally make all these recipes in small batches, you need not fear having to come up with ten extra jars. Usually eight to ten 8-fluid-ounce jars will do. And most of these recipes can be doubled or reduced as desired, with the exception of *jellies.* Jellies should al-ways be made in single batches.

## About Wild Plants

If you are new to the hobby of wild plant cookery, let me make two suggestions:

Make positive identification of a plant before you gather the leaves or fruit for any form of pre-serve. There are a few poisonous plants in every province of this country, and one dare not indulge in indiscriminate brewing and bottling. Write to the Department of Agriculture in your provincial capital, and also ask your county agricultural representative for all free pamphlets about the wild flowers, weeds, shrubs and trees of your prov-ince. And make yourself a present of one reliable wild plant reference book. (For suggestions see p. 132.)

Never pick the last plant. Nature has served us with a lavish hand, and such a legacy brings its own responsibility. Conserve a clump of fid-dlehead ferns, or a bed of fragrant wild ginger, as carefully as if it were your own cultivated perennial border. Take, but do not plunder.

# *Equipment*

Preserving, pickling and wine making require little equipment other than the tools and utensils used from day to day in a reasonably well-equipped kitchen. It is a hobby that can be pursued as successfully in a high-rise apartment as in a spacious country farmhouse.

As with any activity you could think of, our affluent society advertises an overwhelming assortment of gadgets for use in this traditional art which began with a kettle, a rudely carved wooden spoon, and a precious crock for storage. Today there is everything from an electric juicer, to a jelly thermometer, to a hydrometer, which measures the rate of fermentation.

You may enjoy investigating what's available and investing in what appeals to you. But let's begin with a basic list:

- A *cutting board.* You owe it to your counter top.
- *Sharp knives,* large and small.
- *Scissors.* They can snip such things as onion tops, parsley, lemon peel and fresh-picked herb leaves more neatly than knives can.
- A *grater,* fine, and coarse.
- A *food chopper,* or *electric blender.*
- A *food mill,* or *fine strainer,* for reducing soft fruits to puree.
- Crockery, glass, plastic, polyethylene *bowls and jugs.*
- A *large plastic strainer.*
- *Pyrex measuring beakers,* to include a four-cup size with a pouring spout.
- A *rotary hand beater,* or *electric mixer* (portable). Use it just before bottling catsups, chutneys or butters that are not as smooth as you'd like.
- A *wooden mallet,* or *stainless steel potato masher.*
- A long-handled *wooden spoon,* and *silver or stainless steel tablespoons.*
- A rubber or plastic *spatula.*
- A small *plastic funnel.* Invaluable when pouring juices, syrups, wines or vinegars into narrow-necked bottles.
- Crocks. (If you're going to buy some, I suggest getting a one-gallon and a two-gallon size.)
- Clean, worn *linen towels, or tablecloths.* The old-fashioned jelly bag that dripped all night long is not necessary. Pour the cooked fruit into a plastic strainer or sieve, to extract the juice. Then line a fine strainer with clean linen, muslin or any fine cotton, and pour the juice through it, so that it will be perfectly clear.
- A *kettle.* Any large, flat-bottomed saucepan or pot of enamel, aluminum, or stainless steel. Do not use other metals. To remove stain from your aluminum kettle, boil in it for five minutes water to which has been added a couple tablespoons of vinegar and baking soda. It is a good idea to keep a separate saucepan for relishes, chutneys, catsups, and condiments containing onion.
- *Jars.* Preserves require pint or quart jars with rubbers, and metal screw-tops, for a perfect seal, as in canning. But jams, jellies, pickles, syrups and wines can be put into any of the empty jars and bottles you've been saving. Be sure that all jars are shiny-clean, and sterilized.

The simplest method of sterilization is to set the jars in the oven for 10 minutes, at 275 degrees.

- *Parowax.* Keep an old coffee pot or metal kettle with a tight-fitting lid, and use it for this purpose only. When heating parowax, and pouring it, keep the cover on. It is highly inflammable.

Whenever you open a jar of jam or jelly, wash the parowax thoroughly and keep it for re-use. I do not save the wax from chutneys and relishes; for it is virtually impossible to scour out the onion-spice-vinegar odour it absorbs during storage.

# General Hints

Most fruits and vegetables for preserve and pickle should be used as soon as possible after they are harvested. This is especially true when the finished product is to be a crisp pickle or relish.

Wash all fruits and vegetables before cooking. With soft fruits such as raspberries, strawberries, bakeapple, do not run the tap water directly on them; it will crush them out of shape. Instead, place them in a strainer and move it up and down several times in a basin of clean, cold water.

Have your jars in the oven, ready to be sterilized, before cooking begins. If you are using old sealers (for a preserve), test them for a certain seal by filling them with water, setting the rubber rings and the metal tops in place, and inverting them on a dry cloth on the counter.

Simmer fruit gently at first, so it will not stick to the kettle while the juice is beginning to run. Once the sugar is added, boil rapidly.

Stir with a wooden spoon.

To improve the texture of jams, conserves, chutneys and catsups and keep them free of froth and scum, add a tablespoonful of butter. Do not add it to jelly, for it may affect the clarity.

Fill preserve sealers to the very brim. Fill all other jars to within one-quarter inch of the top, and seal with a thin layer of parowax. (Pickles and relishes do not require it. The amount of vinegar in them is adequate preservative.)

Label the jars with name and date. Store them in a cool, dry place, away from bright light.

# *Procedures*

*(Terms in italics are explained in the Glossary.)*

## Beverages

The leaves of herbs and of various wild plants, either fresh-picked or dried, may be brewed to healthful and refreshing **teas.** Brew as you would a cup of China tea, but let it steep twice as long before pouring. A dash of lemon juice will clarify the infusion.

**Fruit and vegetable juices** can be extracted from all surplus produce in season. These juices can then be frozen, canned, or stored in bottles in the fridge. A blender is a boon here; and the soaring price of canned vegetable juices and fruit juices may well justify the purchase, if you don't already own one. Ripe tomatoes, and soft, dead-ripe fruits will yield the necessary liquid when pressed down in the blender container, so their juice or puree, undiluted by the addition of water, is rich in nutritional value.

**Fruit syrups,** made by boiling together fruit juices and sugar, furnish the base for punch, liqueur, children's drinks, and a variety of cocktails both alcoholic and non-alcoholic. Use overripe fruits, for the juice will run more freely. Discard all mouldy or rotten parts. The amount of water added while cooking will vary with the type of fruit. Soft fruits such as strawberries, peaches, loganberries, will require little or no water; while gooseberries, rhubarb, elderberries, rose hips, may require a cup of water for every two cups of fruit. The amount of sugar to be boiled with the extracted juice will vary with personal taste; but a tart, concentrated juice usually requires one-half cup sugar for each cupful of the liquid.

Similarly, the infusion from fresh herb leaves such as mint and sage, and flower heads such as roses, clover, marigolds, and hawthorn bloom, can be boiled with sugar to make syrups that are used as fruit syrups.

**Wines** are a slower process. They demand both patience and time. Today home wine-making is a popular hobby with men and women alike. There are short courses in wine making, wine makers' clubs, and at least two regular national publications that keep devotees of the craft informed about the latest tips and the newest gadgets. The wines in this book do not follow the modern method. They belong to an older tradition – that of cottage, folk, or country wines, which were treasured in this land long before the wine-art process with its array of added chemicals was ever thought of. These wines belong to a time when settlers traded precious recipes brought from their homelands and brewed a part of each harvest into wines that would bring much pleasure when used for social, nutritional, even medicinal purposes in the coming winter months.

True, there is an element of chance in the folk- or country-wine method – a risk that the chemicals in the new scientific method of home wine-making practically eliminate. But the adventure of the older process far outweighs the risk, and there is the added advantage of variety. Once the basic elements of the country method are mastered it is possible to evolve a balanced wine recipe from almost anything that is edible.

The keynote is cleanliness. All fruits, flowers,

foliage and roots should be sound and clean. All kettles, crocks, utensils and bottles should be sterilized before use. Never use metal vessels for fermenting wine, or for stirring or handling it in any way once *fermentation* has begun.

To add the *yeast,* dissolve one package of active, dry yeast with a teaspoon of sugar in a cup of lukewarm water or juice. Many of the early wine recipes let fermentation begin very slowly, without yeast. But I add it to all wines, as early as possible in the process – before the plant's natural wild yeasts have had a chance to become active and cause any trouble.

Wine should be started at a temperature from 70 to 80 degrees; *set away to work* in a cool, dry place from 50 to 65 degrees, and stored after bottling in a dry, dark place that will not heat to above 55 degrees.

To add the sugar, heat a portion of the juice to lukewarm and stir the sugar into it until all is completely dissolved.

The wine recipes included in this book are all for a small quantity of wine, little more than a gallon. Fill the gallon *fermentation jar* to within an inch of the bottom of the glass tube, and if there is liquid left over, put it in a bottle, loosely corked, and use it to keep up the level of wine in the jar as it decreases during fermentation.

A wine should remain in the fermentation jar until it is clear. If there are heavy *lees,* it would be well to pour or *siphon* it off two or three times before the final bottling. If a wine just won't come clear, *fine* it by adding the crushed shell of an egg and letting it rest for 2 or 3 weeks more.

Bottle your red wines in coloured glass; your leaf, flower and herb wines in clear glass. When you are using corks, rather than screw tops, buy new corks each time.

For reference and comparison, the bottle's label should record the date started, the date bottled, and any significant fact you may have noted during the process. Ardent home wine-makers keep notebooks.

## Catsups, Chutneys, Relishes.

All three of these condiments can be made from fruits and vegetables at various stages of growth. Green vegetables, and unripened fruit yield a crisper **relish. Chutneys** are usually treated with hot spices. **Catsups** are made by forcing the cooked fruit or vegetable through a sieve, or making a puree of it in the blender, before vinegar, spices and sugar are added for further boiling. Unlike pickles, which require choice whole vegetables, chutneys, relishes and catsups can be made from fruits and vegetables of irregular shapes and sizes, since all the ingredients are chopped fine anyway.

For a crisp relish, keep the cooking time of the chopped vegetables to a minimum.

Chutneys and catsups should be boiled until they reach a jam-like consistency.

## Conserves, Marmalades, Preserves

A **conserve** is made like a jam, but it contains more than one fruit, and usually maraschino cherries, or nuts, are added near the end of cooking time. Conserves are of a thinner consistency than jams, and it is not necessary to boil them until they test for set.

A **marmalade** includes in its ingredients the peel and juice of at least one citrus fruit.

A **preserve** is a fruit cooked in a rich syrup in such a way as to keep the fruit or pieces of fruit whole and unbroken.

### Jams and Jellies

**Jam** is a fruit boiled with sugar until the fruit has lost its shape and the ingredients are thick enough to test for set. To do this, put a spoonful of the boiling jam on a plate, and cool it. When you move the plate back and forth, if the surface of the cooled mixture wrinkles, the jam is cooked.

The best jams are made from fruit that is slightly under-ripe, for then the pectin content is highest.

Most jams are improved in flavour and consistency by the addition of two or three tablespoons of lemon juice and one of butter.

If you are using commercial pectin for jam, follow the directions given on the package.

**Jellies** require more time to make than do jams and conserves, for the juice has to be extracted from the fruit, and re-strained to be perfectly clear, before the actual jelly-making can begin. But the process is simple, and the results are a delight to the eye as well as to the palate.

I am an enthusiastic convert to the short-boil method of jelly-making, with the use of additional pectin. Otherwise, even the most pectin-rich juice must boil with the sugar for ten or fifteen minutes before it will jell; by that time, much of the fresh-fruit flavour has been destroyed.

Every ripe fruit contains some pectin, a plant substance that acts as a binder for fruit cells and, when combined in proper balance with sugar and the fruit's acid, aids in making the liquid into jelly. Some fruits are high in pectin – for example apples, cranberries, gooseberries, red currants. Others are low – including pears, rhubarb, elderberries, strawberries. Fruits like blackberries, peaches, apricots and raspberries are medium. Some wild fruits, such as barberries, rowanberries and sumac, are extremely high in pectin.

The addition of commercial pectin crystals, adjusted in quantity to the need of each fruit, simply guarantees the balance required for a perfect jelly. Commercial pectin is itself a natural plant product extracted from citrus fruits.

A third advantage. The use of pectin crystals makes it possible to produce delicious savoury jellies from plants, or parts of them, which contain no pectin at all, such as leaves, blossoms, herbs, onions, cucumbers, and celery.

So, all the jelly recipes in this book have been adapted to the use of one package of commercial pectin crystals. *Do not double a jelly recipe,* even if you are fortunate enough to have twice as much fruit as is required. Make two batches. Both jams and jellies are best made in small quantities.

To test a jelly for set, hold a spoonful of the boiling mixture above the kettle and let it drop back into the pot from the side of the spoon. When two drops come together and fall as one, you can be confident that the jelly will set.

Let the jelly stand in the kettle for three minutes after it is removed from the heat. Then, with a silver or stainless steel spoon, remove and discard the sheet of scum that will have formed. Pour at once, and your jelly will be beautifully clear.

The recipes in this book are calculated to yield from five to seven 8-fluid-ounce jars of jelly.

Commercial methods of freezing foods have improved to the point that it is possible to make excellent jams and jellies from store-bought frozen fruit and juices. Measure the fruit before freezing, and label it with the amount. Add no sugar until cooking time.

## Pickles

Although there are excellent standard brands on the market, no commercial product can equal in flavour the tangy pickles produced with leisurely care from treasured early recipes. These recipes come to us from a time when pickles were the only crisp green vegetables to be had throughout the long months of winter, and their skilful preparation was highly regarded as an art.

The primary rule for pickling is freshness. You cannot make crunchy, satisfying pickles from cucumbers, young onions, peppers, green tomatoes that have sat around in baskets for a few days awaiting your attention. Rush the vegetables from the vines to the crock.

Fruits for pickling – green gages, crab-apples, pears, peaches – should be gathered before they are quite ripe.

Use pickling salt, rather than table salt.

Use good vinegar; and whole spices tied in a small square of muslin or linen to make a spice bag. Ground spices will not affect the taste of your pickle, but they will make it look dark and "groundsy".

Pickles should sit in a crockery vessel for salting; they should be cooked only in stainless steel, aluminum or enamel pans; be stirred only with a wooden spoon; and be bottled in glass or stored in a crock.

Pack pickles neatly into glass jars, and pour the vinegar solution almost to the top of the jar. Use screw tops. If the inside of the lid is not lined, make a liner of heavy waxed paper and fit it in; otherwise the vinegar may eat into the metal and affect the taste of the pickle.

No pickles should be made today and eaten tomorrow. Give them at least a month in which to mature.

# Glossary

*Fermentation* – the process by which the action of yeast converts the sugar in a liquid into alcohol and carbon dioxide.

*Fermentation jar* – any sterilized gallon cider or vinegar jar, fitted with a fermentation lock. A fermentation lock is a plastic valve with a short glass tube, and is available for less than a dollar at any wine supply centre. As the wine works in the jar, this device allows carbon dioxide to escape and prevents air and fruit flies from entering.

*Fining* – Sometimes a wine remains cloudy, even after the action has ceased. To fine it, add the crushed shell of an egg, or a spoonful of egg-white beaten into a cup of the wine, and let the wine rest for a few weeks more, before bottling.

*Lees* – the sediment of fruit and yeast particles that sinks to the bottom of the jar during fermentation.

*Puree* – vegetables or fruit reduced to a smooth pulp.

*"Set away to work"* – When the liquid is transferred to the fermentation jar, the temperature may be lowered for the longer, slower second fermentation. The jar should be set in a dry, cool place, with a temperature between 50 and 65 degrees, where it will be undisturbed for a couple of months.

*Rack.* See *siphon.*

*Siphon* – Technically speaking, a siphon is a hose to transfer a liquid from a higher level to a lower level, by gravity. Wine can be poured from the fermentation jar into bottles. But it is simpler to siphon it off with an inexpensive length of plastic tubing, available at a wine supply store. I set the gallon jug of wine on top of a crock on the counter, and place the bottles to be filled in the sink nearby. Little or no wine is lost in bottling with this technique.

*"Test for set."* See both **Jams** and **Jellies,** p. 21.

*Yeast* – microscopic fungus that consumes sugar, producing alcohol and carbon dioxide. There is natural plant yeast on the skin of most ripe plants. But the addition of commercial yeast hastens the action and produces a more violent first fermentation, and it prevents any of the fruit's wild yeasts from taking over and ruining the wine.

Good wines can be made with baker's yeast. But as you become more engrossed in the hobby, you may wish to try various culture yeasts, such as champagne, sauterne, or sherry yeasts. Samples of these may be obtained free of charge from the Horticultural Research Institute of Ontario, Vineland Station. No doubt other provinces have similar sources; contact your provincial Ministry of Agriculture and Food. Of course wine yeasts can also be purchased in a wine supply shop.

# *Apples*

Our history is redolent of apples.

The crab-apple, or wild apple, is native to Canada; so nearly four hundred years ago, when those earliest settlers felled the trees to make homes for themselves in an alien land, they were quite literally, in the biblical sense, "comforted with apples". When spring came at last, after the first barren, bitter winter, what joy it must have been to catch sight of the tight pink buds, the fragrant pale petals, of a wild apple tree, lovely against the dark, impenetrable forest. And until the land was cleared enough for garden plots, what treasure even those sour, acrid little apples must have been to people starved for fruit.

We make use of the wild crab still; for the jelly and the catsup from them is sharper, fuller in flavour than that made from cultivated crab-apples. But its lasting importance lies in the fact that it is a kind of patriarch. From its seedlings have been developed the many different varieties of cultivated fruit that have made Canada a leading apple-producing country.

It is reasonable to suppose that within a few years following the establishment of the first Canadian settlement at Port Royal in 1605, more than one colonist would have transplanted a small wild apple tree or two into his own rough plot. Newcomers brought treasured seeds from their homeland – seeds of the London Pippin, Flower of Kent, Hawthornden, Royal Russet, Cornish Gilliflower, Ladies' Sweeting – and when the small seedlings rooted and grew large enough, they were grafted onto the hardy native apple trees. Not all of the European varieties were suited to this climate. But gradually, with patience and experiment, orchards were established, and many excellent species were developed and given names. By the late 1700s, areas of both Upper and Lower Canada were known to be apple-growing country.

Perhaps the most famous Canadian apple has been the McIntosh Red, named after John McIntosh of Dundas County, bordering the upper St. Lawrence River in Ontario. In 1796 he transplanted a number of wild apple trees; and from the single one that lived and thrived, grafts were distributed to orchards throughout the province. The firm, juicy crimson apples they eventually bore were called McIntosh Reds.

The Snow Apple (Fameuse), produced shortly afterwards in Quebec, is in demand to this day, because of the delicate colour and flavour of Snow Apple Jelly. Other varieties – Jonathan, St. Lawrence, Spartan, Winter Blush, Melba, Wolfe River, Yellow Bellflower, Northern Spy – all became favourites in Canadian orchards. In the 1830s, Samuel Strickland wrote back to England: "The apple tree flourishes in this country and grows to a large size. I gathered last year, out of my orchard, several Ribstone Pippins, each of which weighed more than twelve ounces."

And in 1855, Catherine Parr Traill, in *The Canadian Settler's Guide,* listed thirty-eight varieties grown here, and added: "There are many other capital apples, but these are the most celebrated."

In this climate, where the lack of fresh food was a real hardship throughout the long winters, apples were of inestimable culinary value. Varieties that proved to be "good keepers" were stored in root-houses for winter use. More perishable kinds were dried each autumn to provide a winter's wealth of steamed puddings, pies, fritters and dumplings. Apple butter was a tasty and inexpensive jam. Apple juice and hard cider (Apple Jack) became staple beverages. And the cider, exposed to the air until it turned into vinegar, made possible the pickling of surplus vegetables and fruits.

In many settlements, apple harvest time was a veritable social whirl. The summer's work had left the settlers little time for neighbouring. But now in early autumn they could gather for a leisurely visit while the fortunate owner of a press transformed sacks of apples into barrels or kegs of sweet amber-coloured cider.

Then there was the Paring Bee, where everyone was invited to each house in turn, to peel, core, and string for drying the bushels of apples that were not of a sort to weather long storage in house or root-cellar. Those evenings were happy times for old and young alike. The young men brought their apple-paring machines, and the paring was their part of the process. The men passed the apples along to the young ladies, who quartered and cored them. Then the children used darning needles to string the apple quarters on strong coarse thread; and the tallest men hung the strings of apples on poles, up near the ceiling, to dry in the kitchen warmth. When all the litter had been cleared away, the hostess served gingerbread and sweet cider and apple pie to everyone; and, if the man of the house happened to own a fiddle, there would be a rousing square dance beneath the festoons of apples before the evening ended.

It is a far cry from those first experiments to the huge, glossy apples that make a feast of our fruit-stands today. Yet for jelly and catsup and wine, the crabbed, nameless wild apples are still the best.

## Wild Apple Melomel

When a fruit juice, instead of water, is combined with honey to ferment, the wine is known as a melomel.

4 qts. wild apples, all sizes, shapes and colours
5 qts. water
2-1/2 lbs. liquid honey
yeast

Wash, stem, and quarter the apples and boil them in the water until they are soft enough to mash.

Strain off the juice into a crock, and add the honey, stirring until the honey is completely dissolved.

When cooled to lukewarm, add the yeast. Cover with a thick towel, and stir once each day for 10 days.

Strain through cloth and set away in a cool place, in a fermentation jar, to work for 3 or 4 months. When it is still, bottle it and forget it for 7 or 8 months longer.

## Lamb's Wool

On a winter evening recently, we revived this long-forgotten recipe for a hot toddy. By some it was called Apple Ale, by others, Lamb's Wool.

1 qt. hot ale
1 cup sweetened applesauce
dash of ginger and cinnamon

Stir briskly. Serve just off the boil.

## Apple Butter

The confection which follows is not to be confused with the dark-coloured pure apple butter sold commercially. Rather, it is a rich jam, mellow with brandy and oranges.

The original method has been adapted to the use of a blender.

Wash, core, and quarter firm, tart apples (5 lbs. will leave some over for munching), and in the blender reduce them to apple-sauce consistency. To 5 cups of this puree, add the finely grated rind, and the juice, of 2 oranges and 1 lemon. Cover, and bring slowly to the boil. Stir in 1 cup liquid honey and 3 cups sugar. Boil, and stir, until thick – about 10 minutes. Remove from heat. Stir in 1 tbsp. butter and 3 tbsp. good brandy. Bottle, and seal with parowax.

## Apple Ginger Chutney

This condiment is especially good with a hot curry.

10 large, firm apples – for example, Northern
    Spy, Wealthy, Cortland – cored, and chopped
    coarsely
1 large onion, chopped fine
2 large green peppers, seeded,
    and chopped fine
1 cup dried currants
3 tbsp. salt
juice and grated peel of 1 lemon
1 qt. apple cider vinegar
3 cups brown sugar, tightly packed
1 6-oz. bottle preserved ginger,
    chopped fine, and its syrup
1 tsp. ground cloves
1 tsp. allspice
3 tsp. ground ginger

In a large kettle, bring to the boil, sugar, vinegar, salt and spices. Add peppers, onion, currants, and simmer for 30 minutes. Then add all other ingredients and boil gently, for another 30 minutes, stirring frequently. Bottle and seal.

## Sweet Apple Pickle

There are several versions of this recipe, and they all express preference for Tolman Sweet apples. But we have tried it with small Golden Russets, while they were still firm and crisp, and from now on, the Russet is our choice.

2 cups cider vinegar
2 lbs. brown sugar
1/2 cup water
1 tsp. powdered alum
1 tsp. ground cloves
1 tsp. ground ginger
1 tsp. crushed cardamom
1 tsp. salt

Pare, core, and quarter the apples. Boil the other ingredients together for 5 minutes. This will make enough syrup for about 5 lbs. apples. Cook a small quantity of the apples in the syrup, for only 3 minutes, then pack them into sterilized jars. Add more apples to the syrup, and cook them. When all are cooked and packed, boil the syrup for another 5 minutes, then fill up the jars with it. Seal. Do not serve for at least a month.

This is a rich, sweet, spicy pickle, especially good with meat. When the apples are all eaten, use the remaining syrup to baste a baking ham or oven-browned pork chops.

## Flowering Crab Jelly

All varieties of the flowering crab trees that decorate so many city and suburban lawns yield a jelly that is deeper in colour and fuller in flavour than that made from the regular jelly crab-apple. We have collected the fruit, on occasion, from neighbours who hadn't even realized that it could be used.

4 qts. ripe crab-apples, any size
6 cups water
Simmer for 20 minutes – or until the crabs can be crushed, to strain through cloth.
To 8 cups juice, add 1 pkg. commercial pectin and bring to the boil.
Stir in 9 cups sugar.
Boil until it tests for set. Bottle, with a clove in each jar, and seal with parowax.

# *Apricot*

The apricot tree is native to the Mediterranean countries and China. In only two areas of Canada has it been cultivated successfully – in British Columbia's Okanagan Valley, and, to a lesser degree, in Ontario's Niagara Peninsula.

Years ago when our corner grocery sold dried apricots from a large wooden tub on the counter, Mr. Farmer would pop one into each of our mouths as my brother and I huddled around the scales to see that our mother's pound of dried apricots was never a breath less than 16 ounces.

That ritual treat was better than gum or candy.

"Soak it in your spit," one of us would instruct the other. And further conversation was conducted by way of nods and grunts, while the apricots softened in our closed mouths. Then, all the way home, we'd suck and nibble on the refreshingly acid fruit, which had once looked like a lovely little peach without the fuzz.

Soaked overnight in water to cover them, then combined with an equal quantity of sliced tart apples, a cup of sugar, and a teaspoon of crushed cardamom seed, those wizened apricots were transformed into our mother's mouth-watering Apricot Apple Pie for Sunday dinner.

Today, canned and dried apricots are available everywhere. The dried apricots sold in health food shops are not treated with chemical preservatives and usually have an especially fine flavour.

## Apricot Wine

A *Centennial Year Cook Book,* compiled by the Ottawa branch of the Kingston General Hospital Nurses' Alumnae, features this recipe.

2 20-oz. tins apricots, or 3 qts. fresh apricots
2-1/2 lbs. white sugar
1 lb. light raisins
2 medium potatoes, scrubbed and sliced
4 qts. boiling water

Pour the boiling water over the first four
ingredients, in a crock.
Cool to lukewarm and add yeast.
Stir daily, bruising apricots and potatoes.
After 10 days, strain into a fermentation jar
and set away to work for 3 or 4 months.

Mary McKenzie, who contributed the recipe, added the footnote: "This is quite strong. I was serving it one night and half our guests fell asleep after dinner." Her original version has been altered here to produce a drier, lighter wine, but one not necessarily less potent.

## Apricot Orange Jam

Experimenting recently with frozen juice and a
blender, I evolved from the unpromising-looking
dried apricot this delicious jam.

Soak overnight:

   1  lb. dried apricots in
   6  ozs. frozen orange juice, thawed
      but undiluted.

Next day, whirl in the blender with 2 thin-skinned
oranges and 1 lemon, quartered. To each cupful of
this puree, allow 3/4 cup sugar. Add 1/2 tsp. salt
and 1 tbsp. butter, and boil until thick. Bottle, and
seal with parowax.

This succulent plant was introduced early into Canadian gardens. A cookbook published in Montreal in 1845, entitled *Modern Practical Cookery,* offered an excellent recipe for pickling the tender young asparagus shoots. The following recipe is a simplified version, but equally delicious, and a welcome addition to a party relish tray.

### Pickled Asparagus

Wash 3 lbs. young asparagus spears not more than 3″ in length, and cook them in boiling water for 5 minutes. Drain thoroughly, and pack them in jars, upright. Boil together for 10 minutes:

- 4 cups vinegar
- 1 cup water
- 1 tbsp. salt
- 2 tbsp. sugar
- 1 tsp. each of nutmeg, mace, alum, and white pepper.

Fill up the jars with the boiling-hot syrup. Seal. Do not use for at least a month.

# *Bakeapple*

The bakeapple, or *cloudberry* as it is also called, is a soft, seedy, juicy berry, with the rather mellow flavour of a baked apple and the appearance, when ripe, of a fat yellow raspberry. It grows in bogs and barrens from Nova Scotia to the Yukon, and is plentiful in Newfoundland and Cape Breton.

In Evelyn Richardson's autobiographical *We Keep A Light,* she tells of her first summer on a lonely island:

> In spite of not being well the first summer, I had managed to can and preserve several bottles of berries, particularly raspberries, which grew in great abundance along the path to the boathouse. Morrill and I would put both babies in the carriage and wheel them to the berry patch. . . . Another berry which was plentiful that summer was the luscious swamp berry which we called the baked apple. I could not go to pick these as they grew some distance from the lighthouse and in swampy places where we could not take the babies. . . . We consider them the most delicious berry that grows.

## Bakeapple Jam

A friend in Cape Breton sent us a jar of Bakeapple Jam for Christmas morning breakfast; and included the recipe for it.

3 cups bakeapple berries
2 cups sugar

Place together in a large saucepan and let stand overnight. Next morning, bring berries slowly to the boil, stirring frequently. [I add three tbsp. lemon juice.]

Boil gently for 20 minutes. Pour into hot sterilized jars and seal with parowax.

*Cloudberry*

# *Wild Barberry*

The wild barberry bush is a lovely sight, tucked into a fence corner at the edge of a grainfield, or clinging to a cleft in the rock of a barren hillside. It sometimes reaches a height of eight feet. In early summer the thorny branches bend gracefully beneath a weight of soft yellow bloom; in late autumn the clusters of elliptical, bright red berries provide irresistible wealth to the wine or jelly maker.

Throughout recent years there have been thorough campaigns in some areas to eradicate the wild barberry, since it is host plant for the stem-rust of grain. But barberry is an exceptionally hardy perennial, and no Department of Agriculture has been able to control it completely. Even on hillsides and meadows where weed killer has done its work, a stray bush or two flaunts its coloured harvest each November.

Early settlers to this continent, overcome with nostalgia for the English country gardens of their homeland, referred to the wild barberry as "the poor man's red currant." In colour, and in flavour, barberry jelly closely resembles red currant jelly, but it is tarter. The fruit is highly acid and requires somewhat more than the average amount of sugar.

Unlike the dry, woody, useless berries of your cultivated barberry hedge, wild barberries are tender and juicy.

## Barberry Jam

Remove the berries from their stems. Wash them. Allow 1 cup of sugar for each cup of fruit.

Heat sugar and berries to the boiling point, stirring frequently, and bruising with a wooden spoon. Add 1 tbsp. butter. Boil gently for 20 minutes. Bottle and seal.

## Preserved Barberries

2 lbs. sugar
2-1/2 cups water
barberries on their stems

Boil together the sugar and water for 5 minutes. Simmer the clusters of barberries in this syrup for 30 minutes; then gently lift them from the syrup, without dislodging any from their stems, and pack them in hot sterilized sealers. Simmer the syrup for 10 minutes more, then pour it over the fruit to fill each jar to overflowing. Seal.

In mid-winter, these crimson clusters look luscious on a relish tray, or edging a platter of cold turkey. For a memorable dessert, empty a sealer of Barberry Preserve into your best clear glass serving bowl and fill up the bowl with scoops of vanilla ice-cream.

# Basil

This annual is native to India and the northern Mediterranean countries; but it can be cultivated successfully in moderate climates, and has long been a favourite in Canadian herb gardens.

There are different varieties, most common being the ordinary Sweet Basil. Its aromatic, spicy leaves make herb vinegar. And fresh or dried, they belong in soups and stews; with tomatoes and eggplant, baked fish and lamb; in chilled vegetable juices and green salads.

Several years ago we discovered the Red, or Purple, Basil. We plant a dozen seedlings each year, so that we will have the firm, shiny, dark-red leaves for this jelly.

## Red Basil Jelly

2 cups fresh Red Basil leaves
2-1/4 cups cold water

Bring to the boil, then set aside, tightly covered, for 20 minutes. Strain the infusion through cloth. To 2 cups of it, add:

1/4 cup strained lemon juice
1/4 cup cider vinegar
1-1/2 cups clear apple juice
1 pkg. commercial pectin crystals.

Stir until it boils, then add:

4 cups sugar.

Boil hard for 1 minute. Pour into sterilized jars. When cool, place a fresh red basil leaf in the top of each jar, and seal with parowax.

No colouring is needed in this jelly. When the lemon juice and vinegar are added to the strained infusion, it takes on a beautiful clear-red colour that makes this jelly delightful to look at as well as to eat. Try it with a fluffy cheese omelette, or a platter of cold ham and chicken.

# The Bergamots

Bergamots are members of the Mint family, and all varieties have an odour and taste that is best described as a mixture of sage and mint.

The Red Bergamot – also known as Oswego Tea – grows in marshy thickets and along the banks of quiet streams. It has a handsome scarlet bloom, which looks like a small pin-cushion stuck with thick red pins.

The more common Wild Bergamot is smaller and less showy – shorter stalk, narrower leaves, and a smaller flower, identical in shape and composition to the Red Bergamot, but ranging in colour from very pale lavender, through deep lilac, to red-purple. It is not a marsh plant. In our area of central Ontario, dry meadows, clearings, and open hillsides are mauve with it in early August, and the summer afternoons are filled with the faint scent of sage and the hum of foraging bees – reminding us of the Bergamots' alternate name, *Bee Balm*.

## Wild Bergamot Tea

Early settlers dried the flowers and the foliage of bergamots and used it as a substitute for tea. We make a pleasant, refreshing drink from the fresh-picked leaves.

1 cup fresh bergamot leaves
3 cups boiling water

Pour the boiling water over the leaves. Cover and let steep for 10 minutes. To each cupful of tea, add 1 tbsp. lemon juice and honey to taste.

## Bee Balm Jelly

This jelly is a delicious accompaniment for cold chicken, fish, or cheese and crackers.

2 cups fresh-picked bergamot leaves
2-1/2 cups water

Bring to the boil, then set aside, tightly covered, for 15 minutes. To 2 cups of this infusion (strained through cloth), add:

1-1/2 cups clear apple juice
1/2 cup apple cider vinegar
3 or 4 drops yellow food colouring (optional)
1 pkg. pectin crystals.

Stir until it comes to a rapid boil, then add 4 cups sugar and boil hard for a full minute. When it tests for set, skim, bottle, and cool. Before sealing with parowax, embed a clean bergamot leaf in each jar.

# *Blackberry*

The blackberry is indigenous to Canada. From coast to coast, in fence corners, along roadsides and footpaths, beneath the trees in sprawling old orchards, it bears its sweet, winey fruit. In the barren pasture, the bushes may be only two feet high, and the berries small and quickly dried out by the sun. But in the tangled growth overhanging a stream, or in the shaded thicket at the wood's edge, the thorny blackberry branches may grow to a height of five or six feet, and the berries will be cool and fat and juicy.

There are two different shapes. The *black raspberry* – or *bramble, blackcap, blackberry* – is round, like a common red raspberry, but firmer, and more tightly packed with seeds. The *thimbleberry* – which Catharine Parr Traill, more than a hundred years ago, named the *Canada Blackberry* – is larger, and is shaped like a thimble. Its flavour is tarter than the black raspberry.

To me, there is nothing more completely deep summer than the taste and smell of ripe blackberries with the warmth of the sun on them, or oozing fragrant and deep-crimson from beneath the flaky crust of a pie still hot from the oven. I was just seven years old, the first summer that I spent a week alone, without brothers or sisters, at my Aunt Hannah's farmhouse at the end of a sleepy Ontario side road. Until then, Aunt Hannah had been the aunt whose name could be spelled either forwards or backwards. From that summer on, she was the aunt with whom I picked blackberries every mid-July. We would gather them on the hill behind the milk house, in the cool shadow of the drive-shed, by the worn pasture path the fat cows travelled morning and evening. Then, for one lovely, long afternoon each summer, we'd wander farther afield, to the deserted waste of an abandoned feldspar mine, where round black raspberries spilled over the footpaths and hollows that had once been worn by men and machinery.

The lovely sunlit afternoon was awash with birdsong, the scent of clover bloom, and the gentle sway of pine boughs. Our fingers and our mouths were purple with blackberry juice, and the pails filled more quickly than anyone could hope. We worked to the rhythm of my endless questions, Aunt Hannah's slow, kindly answers, and our comfortable silences. Then it was home with the treasure, to feast on blackberries with thick yellow cream; the rest of the berries would go to make Aunt Hannah's incomparable blackberry pie, jam

laced with lemon peel to cut the sweetness, blackberry butter for wintertime tarts, and a wonderful served-warm-with-cream desert called Blackberry Cobbler.

For me – a fugitive from a crowded household in a gregarious neighbourhood – those blackberry afternoons were sheer delight.

## Blackberry Cordial

In a small town's historical library I came across a cookbook, completely handwritten by a woman who, in 1901, was one of the village's elderly ladies. It contained this recipe for Blackberry Cordial, which has been warming the blood with the very essence of summer for well over a century by now.

Boil blackberries (as many as you can gather), for 5 minutes, crushing and stirring all the while with a wooden spoon. Strain through a sieve, then through cloth. To every pint of the juice, add:

- 1/2 pt. water
- 2 cups sugar
- 1 tsp. each of cloves, mace, cinnamon, ginger and nutmeg.

Simmer for 10 minutes, and re-strain. When cold, add to each pint, 1/2 cup good brandy. Cork tightly and keep in a cool place.

## Wild Blackberry Port

This wine matures quickly and is quite drinkable within 8 months. It is semi-sweet, and a rich, lovely colour in clear glass.

2 qts. ripe blackberries
3 qts. boiling water
2 lbs. sugar
yeast

Crush the berries in a crock, and pour the water over them. Cool to lukewarm and add the yeast. Cover with a thick towel and set in a warm place for 3 days.
Strain off the juice and add the sugar.
Set the fermentation jar away in a cool place for 3 months, in which time the wine should be clear and still and ready to bottle.

## Wild Blackberry Butter

2 qts. ripe blackberries
6 large green apples

Core the apples and slice them into a large preserving kettle. Add the blackberries and crush them until the juice runs freely. Simmer together until the apples are very soft.

Press through a strainer or a food mill; and to each cup of the smooth, seedless pulp, add:

3/4 cup sugar.

Boil until it tests for set.

## Bramble Tip Wine

In earlier times, blackberry leaves were utilized as well as the fruit. The leaves were dried thoroughly in a pan near the fire, then used as a substitute for China tea, which was so difficult to procure in the depths of the Canadian wilderness. The brew was valued doubly when it was discovered to be a remedy for dysentery.

The new foliage of blackberries and raspberries has its uses too; for example, this light, clear, invigorating wine.

In late May or early June, when the blackberries have just come into full leaf, gather 3 qts. of the young leaves. Pour 1 gal. cold water over them and bring it to the boil. Simmer for 20 minutes. Strain, and stir in:

    2 lbs. sugar
    1/2 cup lemon juice
    1 cup light raisins
    when lukewarm, yeast.

Let it work in the fermentation jar for 4 months, then strain, bottle and cork it. Forget it until next time the brambles get new leaves.

## Thimbleberry Jelly

    4 qts. thimbleberries
    2 cups water

Simmer for 10 minutes, mashing the berries with a wooden spoon. Strain through cloth, to yield 4 cups thimbleberry juice.

Add, stirring continuously, 1/4 cup lemon juice and a pkg. pectin crystals.

When it comes to the boil, stir in 4-1/2 cups sugar and boil hard for 1 minute. Bottle, and seal with parowax.

Thimbleberry bushes are taller, and thornier than even the black raspberry. When you go to gather the fruit, go well-protected, wearing gloves and long sleeves.

We like to pick a few of these berries while they are still maroon-coloured, rather than jet-black. It sharpens the flavour of the jelly.

*Thimbleberry*

# Blueberry

Of all our native fruits, the blueberry is probably nature's richest gift to Canada. And it is very definitely a gift, since it is almost exclusively a wild crop – requiring nothing from man but the effort of harvesting it in its yearly abundance. From the Atlantic provinces, across Quebec and Ontario, to the Yukon, blueberries are so prolific that they have become a national product, with a cash crop estimated at nearly four million dollars a year.

They grow on low, matted bushes in bogs and marshes, their lustrous light-blue fruit lovely against the small, shiny-green foliage. They seem to sprout from the very rocks on barren hillsides. And both low and high-bush varieties spring up to cover the soil in burned-out areas of field and woodland.

Year after year, a day's blueberrying, in early August, was one of the ritual joys of summer. With full lunch baskets, empty buckets, running shoes for the rocks and rubber boots for the swampy places, we'd arrive as excited as if it were a holiday, to begin picking as soon as the dew was dried from the bushes. That first hour, every handful of luscious blue fruit that went into the pail was followed by a handful into the mouth. At last, almost drunk on the winey feast, we'd settle down to serious picking.

We never strayed far away from each other; for the hills north of Manitoulin Island and the marshes beyond Kaladar, Ontario, are vast, lonely expanses where one might wander for days without being rescued. Yet, how we envied those families who set up their tent in a shaded spot near the roadside each summertime, and lived in the blueberry country as long as the season lasted, selling each day's harvest to passing motorists.

## Blueberry Conserve

On Nova Scotia's mainland, and on Cape Breton Island, the blueberry harvest is so much a part of the way of life that the province's Department of Agriculture and Marketing offers a booklet titled *Blue Magic,* prepared for distribution by their Home Economics Division. Just to read any one of the forty choice recipes is enough to make one impatient for blueberry season to begin. There are recipes for blueberry pancakes, muffins, fritters; blueberry syrup, wine, cocktail; blueberry jam, jelly and spiced butter. Our thanks to them for this Blueberry Conserve.

1/2 cup water
1 qt. fresh-picked blueberries
sugar
1 lemon, seeded, and sliced paper-thin
1/2 cup coarsely-broken walnuts
1/2 tsp. ground cinnamon

Cook berries and water over low heat, until berries are tender. Measure; and for each cup of berries add 1 cup of sugar. [We reduced this to 3/4 cup because we prefer a tart jam.]

Add remaining ingredients and cook until the jam is thick, stirring frequently to prevent burning.

Pour into sterilized glasses and seal with parowax.

Hi Karen

## Blueberry Jelly

2 qts. fresh-picked blueberries
1/2 cup water

Bring to the boil, crushing the berries with a wooden spoon, and simmer, covered, for 10 minutes. Strain through cloth. To 4 cups juice, add:

1/4 cup lemon juice
1 pkg. pectin crystals

Stir; and when it comes to the boil, add

4-1/2 cups sugar.

Boil for a full minute. Bottle and seal.

## *Spiced Blueberry Jelly*

To the above juice, add 10 whole cloves and 6 cassia buds. Remove them just before bottling.

## *Blueberry and Red Currant Jelly*

Crush, and simmer together for 10 minutes

1 qt. blueberries
1 qt. red currants.

Proceed as for blueberry jelly.

## Blueberry Wine

(From *A Treasury of Newfoundland Dishes*. I recommend yeast, added when you add the prunes.)

To 2 quarts of blueberries add 4 quarts boiling water, and let it simmer until it begins to boil.

Strain, and add 6 cups granulated sugar to a gallon of juice. [If you like a dry wine, reduce the sugar to 4 cups.]

Boil for 5 minutes.

When cool, add 3 cups prunes. Put in a crock; cover with a cloth and let stand for 2 months. Then strain, bottle and cork.

## Huckleberry Pickle

In central Ontario, we refer to the dark-coloured highbush blueberries as *huckleberries*.

3 qts. huckleberries
2 cups brown sugar
1 cup white sugar
1-1/2 cups cider vinegar
1 tsp. each of salt, cloves, allspice
    and cinnamon.

Simmer vinegar and sugar together for 5 minutes. Add berries and spices, and simmer for 15 minutes. Cover the kettle and leave it overnight. Next day, heat to the boil, then pack the berries into sterilized jars. Boil the syrup for 10 minutes, and pour it over the fruit to fill the jars brim-full. Seal.

# Borage

My introduction to this plant happened many summers ago, when I was recently arrived in the neighbourhood, and two elderly ladies invited me to tea. Closing the door on suburbia, where already the sitter was scrambling frantically to meet the demand for pink Freshie and peanut-butter sandwiches, I walked down the road and into another world.

Their house was a spacious, old stone dwelling, where quiet filled the rooms like sweet music, muted colours matched, and the afternoon tea menu featured thin squares of buttered home-made bread. In the centre of each square was a small, star-shaped, beautifully blue flower. It was real. It was to be eaten, they assured me. It was a borage flower.

They had grown the borage in their herb garden, as I have since grown it in mine. It is an annual which seeds itself prolifically; in many areas it grows seemingly wild in waste places, or at the edge of orchards, and in the deserted gardens of abandoned farmhouses. The plant grows to a height of two feet. The leaves are broad, oval-shaped, and very hairy; they have a distinct flavour of cucumber. Pick them as soon as they are full-formed, and add a cupful of chopped borage leaves to your tossed salad.

The deep-blue, star-shaped flowers have the same cucumber flavour as the leaves. They too can be used in salads, or candied, or floated in tall glasses of chilled white wine.

Borage leaves are succulent, and their juice has many pleasant uses. Combined with equal amounts of vinegar and oil, it is an unusual summer salad dressing. Herbalists claim that a borage leaf sweet syrup has all sorts of medicinal values. And it is a delicious hot-weather drink, mixed with chilled tomato juice, or lemonade, or dry vermouth.

## Borage Juice

Whirl in the blender:

  2  cups borage leaves, firmly packed
  1  cup water
  1/4  cup cider vinegar

Keep in covered containers in the refrigerator, and shake well each time before using.


## Borage Jelly

2  cups borage leaves, chopped fine
1/4  tsp. salt
1-1/2  cups boiling water
2  cups clear apple juice
1/2  cup fresh lime juice
1  pkg. pectin crystals

Bring all to the boil and add 4 cups sugar. Boil hard for 1 minute. Remove from heat and let it sit for 15 minutes, stirring frequently. Bottle in sterilized jars and seal with parowax.

This jelly is especially good with fish, or with bread and cheese.

# *Brandied Fruits*

This recipe appears in numerous cookbooks, both ancient and modern, under differing names and with varied methods.

### Brandied Fruits

Half-fill a crock or jar with good apricot brandy. Begin with the season's first fruit; and as each fruit comes into season, toss a cupful into the brandy – fine-chopped young rhubarb, wild strawberries and raspberries, cherries, tart plums, peaches, pears, ripe melon . . .
   Stir well with each addition, and whenever you think of it in between.

Spoon it over ice cream for a party dessert.
   Add it to pineapple jello for an unusual jellied salad mould.
   Line a glass bowl with fingers of light sponge cake. Fill it up with a mixture of diced orange, banana and fresh pineapple. Sprinkle liberally with the brandied fruit, and top with a touch of whipped cream.

# Butternut

In 1615, when Samuel de Champlain became the first white man to penetrate the wilderness of what is now central Ontario, he commented, in his *Voyages,* on the abundance of walnuts.

The Black Walnut and the White, or Gray Barked Walnut (Butternut) are native trees. But no longer are they plentiful in most areas; they have been cut down by the thousands, over the years, for their valuable wood. Some old homesteads still cherish a cultivated English walnut tree. But, although they once grew in such abundance, the native trees are so few, in many regions, that when one is discovered, its location must be marked, mentally, for future use.

## Pickled Butternuts

Pickled Walnuts, when sold commercially, are priced to be a delicacy for special occasions. But you can produce your own at very little cost, if you can locate a Black Walnut or Butternut tree – and if you have patience. There are many old recipes for Pickled Butternuts, which differ widely in both method and ingredients. But on this one point there is unanimous agreement: you can't make them today and serve them come Saturday's supper-party. It takes time.

Gather the green butternuts (or walnuts) from mid-June to early July, before the shell starts to harden. (If you can push an ice-pick through, it is just the right age.)

Pierce each one.

Pour boiling water over them, and towel off the outside fuzz. (For this process, wear rubber gloves, and use paper towels or an old bath towel.) Cover with water, and boil until the water is thoroughly discoloured. Pour off, add fresh, and boil again. Repeat, until the boiled water is clear.

Pack the nuts in sealers or jars. To each jar, add, as you pack,

> 1 dill flower, 3 butternut leaves, 1 tsp. mixed pickling spice, 1/2 tsp. powdered alum,
> 1 tsp. horseradish, 1 tsp. salt, 1 tsp. ginger.

Fill each jar brim-full with boiling-hot cider vinegar. Seal. Set away, and do not serve for at least 8 months, preferably a year.

# Canadian Capers

The small jars of tiny capers sold in Canadian food stores are probably imported from France or Sicily, since the plant is cultivated there for export. It is a trailing shrub, native to countries bordering the Mediterranean. The unopened flower buds are pickled in vinegar.

We have at least one cultivated, and three wild plants, which can be used in the same way. Each tastes different from the other, and not one has the same flavour as the imported caper. But they are every bit as tasty, added to Drawn Butter Sauce, or to cucumbers in sour cream; or served on the relish tray as a pickle.

The bright yellow- or red-flowered trailing garden plant commonly known as the *Nasturtium* has long been valued for culinary use, as well as for the beauty it lends to the garden from mid-July until the first heavy frost. Both leaves and flowers, added to a green salad, give it a cresslike flavour. And the young green buds can be pickled and bottled as capers. More than a hundred years ago, the Domestic Economy section of the August 1869 issue of the *New Dominion Monthly,* printed in Montreal, featured a recipe on how to pickle nasturtiums:

> Prepare a pickle by dissolving one ounce and a half of salt in a quart of pale vinegar, and throw in the young buds as they become fit from day to day.

In early summer, when the creamy head of the *Elderflower* (see p. 64), matures to a cluster of tiny hard green berries, these can be pickled and used as capers. Wait until the berries are fully formed but not quite ready to ripen.

Every May, almost every province has swamps, river sides and meadows that are startlingly lovely with the bright yellow flowers of the *Marsh Marigold.* Its leaves can be cooked as greens and served with melted butter and a dash of lemon juice. Before the flowers open, each one is a tightly closed, firm green bud, slightly smaller than a pea. They too may be pickled.

If you live in the rocky coastal areas of Nova Scotia or British Columbia, you will be able to make use of *broom buds.* This wild plant, with its small leaves, and larger yellow flowers shaped like pea-flowers, is seldom found inland in Canada.

*Only the buds and flowers of broom are usable.* The black seeds and their pea-like seed pods are considered poisonous. But the flowers make a gentle wine; and the buds can be pickled and used as capers.

## Canadian Capers

Pour boiling water over 1 qt. marsh marigold buds, broom buds, fully-formed green elderberries, or young green nasturtium pods.

Simmer gently for 5 minutes, then drain thoroughly, and pack in sterilized jars.

Boil together for 10 minutes:

1-1/2 cups vinegar
1/2 cup water
1 tbsp. sugar
1 tsp. each of salt, celery seed, and ground mustard seed
1/2 tsp. powdered alum.

Fill up the jars brim-full with this boiling syrup. Seal, and store for several weeks before using.

# Cherry

Many years ago, when we bought our Stone House above the Maitland River in Huron County, Ontario, the charm of the century-old farmhouse was at least doubled for us by the presence, just inside the gate, of a huge, ancient cherry tree. Our very own cherry tree! Even if its fruit-bearing days were over, that place just above fence-level, where the big trunk separated into three, would be perfect for a tree house. And the hammock could swing between the tree and the fence post.

But its fruit-bearing days were not over. Not every summer, but perhaps one summer in three, that tree would produce a wealth of fruit to make those summers unforgettable. The birds never had a chance. Three children and their friends were up the long ladder as soon as the first fat cherries turned crimson; it seemed that the tree was never without a human occupant until the harvest ended. Before our youngest was two years old, she managed to climb the ladder to the first loaded bough and balance with one hand while reaching out with the other hand for cherries to stuff into her mouth. Then, while we stood speechless in the gateway, she leaned over a rung, in imitation of the older children, and spit her mouthful of cherry stones into the grass beneath.

Huron County must have been cherry orchard country sometime in the past. For now there is a large number of half-wild cherry trees – juicy sour-reds, the large sweet blacks, and the yellow-pink fruit reminiscent of cultivated English cherries. Throughout those summers we made jelly, jam, wine, preserve, and cherry syrup with the abandon that comes of boundless affluence; but the cherries tasted best of all fresh from the branches.

Not so with our native wild cherries. Most of them are unpalatable as a raw fruit; but for jelly and wine they are far superior in flavour to the cultivated varieties. No province is without at least one of the following species, and many areas have all:

- *Native wild black cherry (Whisky Cherry)*. Large tree; small, rather bitter fruit found in clusters called *racemes*. Each cherry is about the size of a blueberry, and jet-black.
- *Pin Cherry*. In dry, sandy soil, from Newfoundland to British Columbia. Trees slender. Fruit very small, bright red, and has a large seed.
- *Chokecherry*. Fruit, about the size of a pea, grows on racemes like the native black cherry. Size varies from a low shrub to twelve feet. In lanes, roadsides, meadows – everywhere in Canada. Not pleasant to eat raw – catches in the throat. But excellent for wine and jelly and chokecherry vinegar.
- *Sand Cherry*. A low shrub, found in central Canada, in sandy areas and gravelly riverbanks. Deep red fruit is largest of the wild cherries.

## Jean McKee's Chokecherry Wine

This is a dry wine, and the best chokecherry wine I have ever tasted.

3 lbs. chokecherries
1 lb. dark raisins
3 lbs. white sugar
1/2 cup lemon juice
1/2 cup strong, fresh-made tea
1 pkg. all-purpose wine yeast

Wash the ripe chokecherries. Fill a 1 gal. jug with hot water. Measure 2 cups of it into the blender, and add chokecherries. Blend, and empty into a crock. Repeat with measured water and cherries until all are blended. Do likewise with the raisins, then add the remaining hot water to the sludge in the crock.

Add the sugar, lemon juice, tea, and lastly, the yeast. Place the crock in a warm place and stir well with a wooden spoon daily, for 6 days.

Strain through a piece of fibreglass screening, available at the hardware store.

Pour the strained liquid into a gallon jug, making sure the liquid is to the neck of the jug.

Top with a fermentation lock, or a small piece of plastic fastened with a rubber band. Rack in 3 weeks, with siphon tube, and again in 3 months. Bottle when clear, and store in a cool place for at least 1 year.

*Chokecherry*

## Cherry Bounce

Most versions of the old recipe that follows make use of our native wild black cherries, known in many localities as Whisky Cherries. The tall trees were valued for timber, so in most areas of eastern Canada they are now anything but plentiful. Whisky Cherries ripen late. We have gathered them, at the Stone House, on Labour Day weekend.

To every quart of wild black cherries, add a cup of water. Bring to the boil, simmer gently for 5 minutes, then pour into a crock. Mash several times each day, for 3 days, then strain off the juice. To each pint of juice, stir in 1/4 cup sugar, 1/2 tsp. each cloves and cinnamon, and 1 pint good whisky or rum.

Bottle. In 2 months it will be mellow enough to drink – on special occasions and in limited servings.

The above is a simplified method. In many cases, the directions in the original recipe required the whisky to "steep" on the cherries for months.

## Pickled Cherries

Choose choice cultivated sweet cherries, large and firm, with the stems left on. Wash them, and spread to dry on a towel. Half-fill pint sealers with the cherries. Sprinkle a teaspoon of sugar in each jar, then fill the jars with cherries. To each jar, add:

1 tsp. salt and
1/2 cup white vinegar.

Fill the jars to overflowing, with cold water, then seal. Store in a cool dark place for several months.

## Wild Cherry Jelly

2 qts. wild black cherries, pin cherries, chokecherries, or sand cherries
3 cups water

Bring to the boil, mashing and crushing cherries. Cover and let simmer for 15 minutes. Strain through cloth, to obtain 4 cups juice.

Add 1 pkg. pectin crystals and heat to boiling. Stir in 4-1/2 cups sugar, and boil hard for 1 minute. Bottle, and seal with parowax.

# Ground Cherry

The Ground Cherry (sometimes called the *Husk Tomato*) is not a cherry at all. The plant is sprawling and low, about a foot high, and is a member of the Nightshade family. The ripe fruit is a round yellow berry, about the size of a cultivated cherry, firm and shiny-skinned, wrapped in a papery, light-brown husk. In areas of southern and eastern Canada they grow wild, in fields and in among the corn and melons. Now and again we find them on a market, in early autumn, but few people cultivate them any more. That is a pity, for ground-cherry preserve and jam have an exotic flavour all their own, and ground-cherry pie, with lemon peel and a sprinkle of crushed cardamom, is a memorable delicacy.

## Ground Cherry Jam

Husk 1 qt. ground cherries and bruise them in the jam kettle with a wooden spoon. Grate in the peel of 2 lemons, and add the juice. Simmer, covered, for 5 minutes.

Add 1 pkg. pectin crystals and bring to the boil. Stir in

  4  cups sugar
  1  tbsp. butter

Boil for 1 minute, or until it tests for set.

# *Citron*

Whenever I manage to find citrons for sale at a wayside fruit stand in early autumn, invariably the gardener remarks, "People seldom ask for citrons any more."

I suppose not. Unlike melons, they cannot be eaten uncooked, and they are not the simplest fruit to prepare for the preserving kettle. But citron was the fruit of my childhood winters, when in an area not abundant with other fruits, every back garden on our street had its own citron patch, and the most frequent winter-time dessert was ginger cookies and citron preserve. My mother served it chilled; and it was cool and fresh after the hot meat course.

Then there was my aunt's Citron Marmalade, and a Citron Jam with ginger in it. They seem to have disappeared (although Evelyn Robertson makes a Citron Delight, an updated version of the old conserve, which she sells at Toronto's Black Creek Pioneer Village).

There was Citron Wine, limpid and cool-looking, and a steamed Citron Pudding with mace in it, and a Citron Cake that was rich and moist and tasted of brandy.

Perhaps – although we children were unaware of it – citron was a Depression fruit, in those days when the price of out-of-season fruit was prohibitive. Yet, even today, I find Citron Preserve with ginger cookies every bit as satisfying a dessert.

## Citron Wine

This is a dry, light wine.

4 qts. ripe citron, sliced
1 gal. boiling water
1/2 cup lime juice
1 cup raisins
2 lbs. sugar
yeast

Pare and seed the citron, and slice it, dice it, or do it in a blender. Put the citron pulp in a crock, with the raisins, and pour the boiling water over it. Cover it with a cloth. Stir and mash daily, for 5 days. Strain into the fermentation jar and add the lime juice, sugar, and yeast. Set the jar away from early autumn until springtime, then bottle the clear wine.

## My Mother's Citron Preserve

Quarter the citrons, remove peel and seeds, then slice the fruit and dice it to make 10 cups. (My mother's cubes were about a quarter of an inch. Sometimes we helped, and then the size varied considerably.)

Cover it with a weak brine made by adding 1 tsp. salt to each quart of cold water, and let it stand overnight.

Next day, drain the citron thoroughly, and add it to a syrup made by boiling together for 5 minutes:

    4 cups sugar
    3 cups water.

Cook until the citron is tender, and transparent. Add:

    1 cup raisins,
    10 cloves,
    2 lemons, sliced very thinly,

and cook 5 minutes longer. Remove the cloves. Bottle in sterilized sealers.

# *Clover*

Several species of clover grow wild in meadows and roadsides across Canada. The plants differ in size and appearance, and their flowers may be white, yellow, mauve, pink, or a deep rose-red. But no variety is harmful; in fact, first the native peoples, then the early settlers, used the plant medicinally. From red clover blossoms, mixed with the bark and leaves of other wild plants, they produced a cough medicine, which was used widely until more sophisticated remedies became available. And long after Clover Tea ceased being drunk as a spring tonic, it was brewed from dried clover flowers and mint leaves, to be enjoyed as a pleasant beverage.

We have used the fresh red clover bloom, and fresh-picked mint, or wild bergamot leaves to make this syrup, which is a pleasant and colourful addition to soda water, lemonade, or a dry white wine.

## Clover Honey Syrup

1 qt. fresh-picked red clover heads
A handful of fresh-picked mint or
   wild bergamot leaves
1 qt. boiling water

Cover tightly, and simmer gently for 5 minutes. Let steep, covered, for another 20 minutes. Strain the infusion through cloth, and add

1 pt. liquid clover honey

Boil together for 3 minutes. Bottle and cork. It will keep indefinitely in the refrigerator. Use 2 tablespoons to a glass.

## Pink Clover Mead

This mead (honey wine) can be made quite as successfully with the deep-red clover bloom. But we especially like the delicate colour which results when the smaller, round, very pale pink clover heads are used.

3 qts. pink clover heads
1 gal. water
2 lbs. clover honey
2 lemons
1/2 cup strong, fresh-made tea
yeast

Pour the water over the clover bloom, in a kettle. Bring to the boil and simmer gently for a half-hour. Strain this infusion onto the honey, thin-sliced lemons, and tea.

Cool to lukewarm and add yeast.

Let it work in the fermentation jar for 3 months, by which time it will be a clear lovely pink, and ready to bottle.

## Rose and Clover Jelly

Rose and Clover Jelly is a delight to the eye – clear, and a beautiful rose colour, which will vary slightly, depending on the kind of roses and the freshness of the clover blossoms. Both should be picked at the height of their bloom, before the colour has begun to fade.

On a dry, sunny afternoon, gather 1 qt. deep-pink or red rose petals, and 1 qt. red clover heads. Eliminate all stems and leaves.

Pour 3 cups cold water over the bloom. Cover tightly and bring to the boil. Remove from heat and let it steep, covered, for 15 or 20 minutes.

In the jelly kettle, combine 2-1/2 cups of this infusion, strained through cloth with

1/4  cup strained lemon juice
1-1/2  cups canned apple juice
1  pkg. commercial pectin.

Bring to a full boil and add

4  cups sugar.

Boil hard for 1 minute. Skim and bottle. When cool, set a rose petal in the top of each jar. Seal with parowax.

This is not a tart jelly. It has a delicate flavour that makes it a perfect accompaniment to hot buttered tea biscuits.

# Cranberry

The cranberry family has several relatives living in Canada from Newfoundland to British Columbia. Some grow in the marshes, some on the barren headlands. In spite of differences in name and appearance, each variety of the fruit is edible, acid, and a shade of red when fully ripe. All can be made into delicious wine, jelly and jam, as well as tarts, cakes and batter puddings.

The low-bush Bog Cranberry, which is sold commercially, still grows wild in Ontario, Quebec, and Nova Scotia. Much more abundant is the High Bush Cranberry, which grows along streams in wooded areas, sometimes to a height of nearly twelve feet. The leaves rather resemble a small maple leaf; and the clusters of juicy berries, which ripen in October, are bright red, little more than half the size of the commercial fruit, and each berry contains a single large flat seed. For this reason it is best used in jelly and wine rather than in sauces and conserves. In cooking, this fruit has a pungent, gamey odour, which some people find unpleasant.

In suburban lawns and gardens there is a cultivated shrub similar in appearance to the native High Bush Cranberry. But when fully ripe its berries are more crimson than bright-red, and they are too bitter to be of any use.

Other common varieties are:

- *Foxberry.* Mountain cranberry, gathered on the rocky open cliffs of the Nova Scotia coastline. "They can be picked far into the winter, if you don't mind freezing your fingers," a friend tells me. And she adds, "I haven't seen foxberries sold in the stores lately. But Mom remembers that they bought foxberries at the grocery store often. The grocer would keep them covered with cold water in a vat. You would bring your own container, and the grocer would scoop the foxberries out of the vat or barrel."

- *Mossberry.* Cranberry-like fruit of northwestern Canada.

- *Partridgeberry.* Newfoundland's cranberry or foxberry.

- *Squashberry.* Similar to the High Bush cranberry. Found in northern swamps from Labrador to Alaska.

- *Pomme de Terre.* A Quebec name for the rock cranberry.

*Squashberry or High Bush Cranberry*

## Wild Cranberry Jelly

4 qts. wild cranberries, crushed,
  and simmered in
4 cups water, to yield
7 cups juice. Strain through cloth.
Stir in 1 pkg. commercial pectin and
bring to a full boil.
Add 8 cups sugar, and boil for 1 minute.
Bottle, and seal with parowax.

This jelly has a sharp, strong flavour. Try it with hot roast beef.

## Cranberry Conserve

1 lb. cranberries
1/2 cup water

Cover. Bring slowly to the boil and cook for 3 minutes. Add

1 medium tin crushed pineapple
juice and shredded peel of 3 lemons
4 cups sugar
1/3 cup chopped pecans
1 tbsp. butter

Stirring frequently, simmer gently for 20 minutes. Bottle, and seal with parowax.

## Cranberry Chutney

1 lb. cranberries
1 large onion, apple, green pepper, orange and
  lemon, done in the blender, or chopped fine
1 cup cider vinegar

Boil all together gently, until soft. Then add:

1-1/2 cups brown sugar
1 tsp. salt
2 tsp. ground ginger
1/2 tsp. each cloves, cinnamon, cayenne,
  and black pepper

Simmer until thick – about an hour – stirring frequently. Bottle and seal.

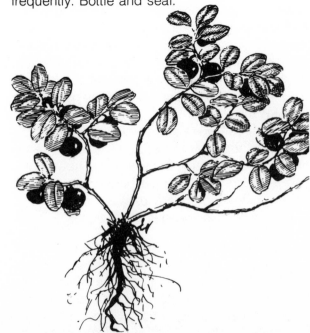

*Mountain or Rock Cranberry*

# Cucumber

To select a half-dozen cucumber recipes for this book was not an easy task. There are thousands of them; they have been accumulating in one country and another ever since Moses led his people into the wilderness and in their hunger they wailed, "We remember the fish we ate in Egypt for nothing; the cucumbers ..." You can make cucumber vinegar and catsup, cucumber pickles and relishes, cucumber soup, cucumber salad, cucumbers in sour cream and caraway, cucumber sandwiches on paper-thin slices of home-made bread and herb butter.

Cucumbers have been cultivated in Canada for more than three hundred years. Seed from Britain and from the American colonies was grown here successfully. In 1824, Reverend William Bell, who had emigrated from Scotland to what is now Ontario's Lanark County, wrote in his *Hints to Emigrants:*

Few kinds of garden stuffs will succeed the first year, as the ground is not sufficiently cultivated. Melons and cucumbers, however, will, and so come to great perfection in this country. They are very refreshing during the great heats in summer and ought to be attended to by all new settlers.

Surely the most historic recipe for pickling the cucumber must be that given by Huron County's colourful William "Tiger" Dunlop, who had come to Canada in 1812, and undertook, some years later, to offer advice to new settlers on the subject of Canadian cookery. In his *Statistical Sketches of Upper Canada,* we read:

Select for this purpose cucumbers the size of a man's foot – if beginning to grow yellow, so much the better; split them in four, and put them into an earthen vessel – then cover them with whiskey. The juices of the cucumber, mixing with the alcohol, will run into the acetous fermentation, so you make vinegar and pickles both at once; and the pickles will have that bilious, Calcutta-looking complexion and slobbery, slimy consistence so much admired by the Dutch gourmands of this country.

You're on your own with William Dunlop's recipe, for I haven't tested it. But the recipes that follow have been tested many times, throughout several generations.

## Aunt Min's Cucumber Salad

We had an aunt named Minnie Mulligan. Her zest for life provided much of the mirth of our early years – added to which, she was a wonderful cook. Even in that Ottawa Valley town of four thousand people, she was such a cook that when all the other denominations met in ecumenical accord at the crowded tables of the Presbyterians' renowned fall suppers, Baptists and Roman Catholics alike were known to ask for Mrs. Mulligan's Marble Cake, or Mrs. Mulligan's Chocolate Meringue Pie.

Since there were only two Mulligan children, as opposed to six of us, her cookie jars and cake boxes were never empty; and we squabbled endlessly over whose turn it was to take a message to Aunt Min's. My brothers drooled over her sticky buns and iced banana cake. But even then my taste was for the sour; one of the recurring pleasures of my young life was to have her seat me at the kitchen table, spread a slice of bread with butter, and ladle into a fruit dish at least half a cupful of a mustard pickle she called Cucumber Salad. My Uncle Bill's eyes would twinkle as he watched me eat.

"Child, you'll shrivel up your stomach with all that pickle," he'd say.

She would grin at him recklessly and add another spoonful to my dish.

In the years since, I have tried many versions of this recipe, but none quite equals Aunt Min's.

Chop coarsely, or dice, all vegetables, to measure:

- 1 qt. cucumbers (small, fresh-picked, firm, and unpeeled)
- 1 pt. onions
- 1 pt. celery
- 1 pt. green pepper
- 1 pt. cauliflower.

Add 3 cups brown sugar, 2 tsp. salt, 1 tsp. powdered alum, to 1 qt. vinegar and bring to the boil.

Add the chopped vegetables, and stir in a paste made of:

- 3/4 cup flour
- 1 tbsp. dry mustard
- 2 tsp. tumeric
- 1 tbsp. celery seed
- 1 tbsp. grated horseradish, and water enough to mix it smooth.

Keep stirring until it comes back to the boil, and thickens. Then simmer it gently for only 3 minutes more, before bottling.

## Cucumber Catsup

A cookbook published in 1911 by the Ladies' Aid of The Christian Church, Newmarket, Ontario, contains this excellent recipe.

Grate the cucumbers (large, unpeeled, and still unripened) and for each quart allow 2 cups vinegar, 4 tbsp. grated horseradish, 2 tsp. salt, and 1/2 tsp. cayenne pepper, and bottle without cooking. [We use the blender for this, instead of the grater; and fresh-ground black pepper instead of cayenne.]

As well as enhancing meat and fish dishes, this catsup is the base for an unusual

### *Salad Dressing*

Combine 1 tbsp. salad oil, 1 tbsp. lemon juice, and 3 tbsp. cucumber catsup.

## Cucumber Lime Jelly

Delicious with cold fowl and fish.

In the blender, put:

    1/2  cup lime juice,
    1/4  cup cider vinegar,
    2  limes, quartered

Blend. Keep adding pieces of firm, fresh-picked, peeled cucumber, and blend, to measure 4 cups in all.

Empty the contents of the blender into the jelly kettle, and add:

    1/4 tsp. salt
    1  pkg. commercial pectin

and bring to the boil. Stir in

    4 cups sugar.

Boil hard for 1 minute, or until it tests for set. Pour into sterilized jelly jars and seal with melted parowax.

## Cucumber Ginger Pickle

The following is a slightly updated version of an old recipe, which obviously originated in an area where people cultivated herb gardens. It can be made without the herbs; but having tried it both ways, I judge the early recipe superior.

8 cups small cucumbers, peeled, and sliced about 1/8 inch thick.
1 cup small onions, sliced
1/2 cup salt
water to cover

Marinate overnight. Next day, drain thoroughly. Make a syrup of:

1-1/2 cups sugar
2 cups vinegar
1 6-oz. bottle preserved ginger
1 tsp. powdered alum
6 each basil, thyme, and marjoram leaves, chopped fine. [I use the scissors.]
1 tsp. celery seed
1 tsp. allspice
3 tsp. ground ginger

Boil for 3 minutes. Add cucumbers and onions, and simmer for 3 minutes more. Bottle and seal.

## Stone House Dills

Wash whole, firm, fresh-picked cucumbers 2 to 3 inches long, and pack them into sterilized sealers, including in each jar:

1 large sprig of dill,
1/2-doz. wild bergamot or thyme leaves, and
3 wild grape leaves.

Make a brine of

2 qts. water,
1/2 cup vinegar,
3 tbsp. salt,
1 tsp. garlic salt,

boiled together for 3 minutes. When it is cool, pour it over the cucumbers to overflowing and top the sealers.

Do not use for at least 2 months.

## Gwen Durst's Nine Day Pickles

Many summers ago, when I first tried this next recipe, I reasoned: "Surely all this fiddling around for nine days isn't necessary." But after several experiments, I know that it is, if the pickles are to taste like Gwen Durst's – rich, sweet, spicy, and crunchy.

The process is not nearly as tedious as it sounds. And the finished product is worth every minute of it.

Wash 4 qts. firm young cucumbers and cut them into chunks. Let stand in salt brine (1/2 cup pickling salt to 1 qt. water) for 3 days. Drain.

Keep covered with cold water for 3 more days, changing the water daily and adding 1 tbsp. powdered alum to it each time. On the 7th day, drain well, and simmer gently for 1 hour in a weak vinegar solution (1 cup vinegar to 4 cups water) to which 1 tbsp. alum has been added.

Drain, and pack into sterilized jars.

Also on the 7th day fill up the jars with this syrup, made by boiling together for 5 minutes:

    4  lbs. white sugar
    3  pts. vinegar
    1  tbsp. powdered alum
    1  oz. celery seed
    1  oz. whole allspice
    1  oz. cassia buds.

Drain off the syrup and reheat it to boiling on the 8th and 9th days. Refill jars with it each time.

Bottle and keep for several weeks before serving.

Small pickling onions (whole), may be added to the cucumbers, if desired.

# Currant

Black and Red Currants are native throughout Canada. Both the Indians and the early settlers dried them for winter use in food and medicine. They may be plentiful still in the moist woods of some localities; but I have never found them in a quantity sufficient for use, so I resort to the cultivated variety when it appears in mid-summer. The wild shrub is similar in appearance, but the fruit is smaller and less juicy.

## Red Currant and Honey Jelly

3 qts. red currants, simmered until soft in
3 cups water, to make
5 cups currant juice, when strained through cloth.

Stir in 1 pkg. pectin crystals, and bring to a full boil. Add 3 cups sugar and 2 cups honey. Boil for 1 minute. Bottle, and seal with parowax.

## Black Mead

2 lbs. ripe black currants
3 qts. boiling water
2 lbs. dark liquid honey
yeast

Bruise the currants in a crock and pour the water over them.

Cover, and leave for 3 days, stirring and bruising daily. Strain off the juice and bring it to the boil with the honey. Boil for 1 minute. Cool to lukewarm, add the yeast, and set it away in the fermentation jar for 3 months, then siphon it off into bottles.

For a comforting negus, or hot drink, on a winter night, add a slice of lemon and a dash of cloves and ginger, and heat it to just under a simmer.

## Red Currant Jelly and Jam

(From Selected Recipes section of the *New Dominion Monthly,* August 1869)

Boil together for exactly 8 minutes some quite ripe red currants of the first quality with an equal weight of sugar. Keep stirring all the time, and clear off the scum as it rises; then turn the preserve into a very clean sieve and put into small jars the jelly which runs through it.

The currants which are left in the sieve make an excellent jam.

One can't have it both ways – but "the currants which are left in the sieve" also make a delicious dessert, baked in a flaky pie with a lattice crust.

# *Dandelion*

Last spring I was astounded to see *Dandelion* among the packets of seed for sale in our local hardware store. Having two lawns in which they grow in wild abandon, I found it a bit ludicrous that anyone should plant them. But the fact that we should be urged to cultivate the dandelion and cook its leaves as we would spinach was evidence of the esteem in which the plant is held.

For centuries this common weed has been valued medicinally in the treatment of everything from kidney ailments to jaundice. Buds, blossoms and leaves all are edible; and in the 1800s, when imported coffee was seldom available, a quite passable substitute was found in the roasted root of the dandelion.

A thick cookbook could be compiled of dandelion wine recipes alone. They have been passed down from one generation to another, like family heirlooms. Some are elaborate – with all sorts of additions such as bananas, dates, herbs, figs, spices. In her book *Country Wines,* Mary Aylett tells of a very powerful dandelion wine, which was "fed" with sugar-candy for one year, then stored for twenty.

My aunt's dandelion wine followed a very simple recipe included in a booklet compiled by Fleischman's of Canada in 1915 that is now a valued item in my collection.

## Dandelion Wine

Pour 1 gallon boiling water over 3 qts. dandelion flowers.* Let stand 24 hours. Strain and add 5 lbs.† light brown sugar, juice and rind of 2 lemons, juice and rind of 2 oranges. Let boil 10 minutes and strain. Cool, and add yeast. After it stops working, bottle it, with a raisin in each bottle. Cork tight.

*A word of caution not included in the original instructions: be careful to use only the yellow blossom, discarding all green, or your wine will have a bitter taste.
†Long ago I changed the 5 lbs. sugar to 3 lbs.

# *Elderberry*

In spite of weed spray and bulldozers, the wild elder is a prolific shrub, still found in meadows and lanes; and it can furnish you with a dozen different delicacies. (We have previously discussed how to pickle the bud of the elderflower, *see* Canadian Capers.)

You will know the elder in late May and early June by its foamy clusters of cream-coloured blossom, which can be turned into elderflower fritters, muffins, tea, vinegar, wine and jellies. In late summer and early autumn, when the small purple-black berries hang in heavy clusters, they can be gathered easily, and used for fruit pies, wine, syrup, jelly and catsup. Elderberry pie requires a generous sprinkle of lemon juice and the grated lemon peel. And the elderberry jelly is improved by the addition of wild grape, mountain ash, or sumac juice.

## Frontignac Wine

The 1845 edition of *Modern Practical Cookery* offers a recipe for wine made with elderflowers. I have scaled it down to manageable quantities, and replaced the "sirip of lemon" with fresh lemon juice.

1 gal. boiling water poured over
2 qts. fresh-picked elder bloom, in a crock.
Stir in 2 lbs. sugar,
1 lb. chopped raisins
1/2 cup lemon juice.
When lukewarm, add the yeast. Let stand, covered with a cloth, for 10 days, stirring daily. Strain, and keep in the fermentation jar for 3 months. Bottle.

## Elderflower and Rhubarb Jelly

Chop red rhubarb to measure 2 qts., and boil it until soft, in water to cover, along with 6 large heads of elder-bloom.
Strain and measure
4 cups juice.
Stir in 1 pkg. pectin crystals and bring to a full boil.
Add 4-1/2 cups sugar and boil until it tests for set.
Bottle, and seal with parowax.

## Elderberry Wine

4  qts. ripe elderberries
4  qts. water
3  lbs. sugar
1/2  cup lemon juice
yeast

Gather the berries on a sunny day when flavour is at its peak. Strip them from the stems and simmer gently in the water for 15 minutes. Strain the liquid into a fermentation jar. Add sugar and lemon juice, and, when lukewarm, the yeast. Set away to work for 2 or 3 months. Bottle when clear.

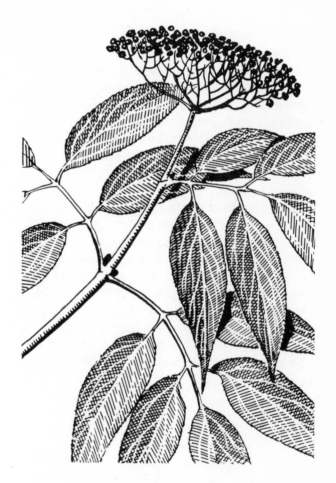

# Fiddleheads

Sometime around the third week of each May, the river beyond our Stone House ebbs back from the flooded marshland and leaves us a bountiful harvest of fiddleheads. These ferns, which in midsummer are luxuriant and waist-high, grow out of last year's root, just at ground level, leaf tightly rolled up into what looks like a green coat-button. They should be picked when the stem is not more than a couple of inches high, before the leaf has begun to unfold.

What a sense of wealth it gives us – to be able to feast to our hearts' content on this succulent delicacy so outrageously expensive at the frozen foods counter. For two full weeks we eat fiddleheads twice a day – boiled and served with lemon juice and a liberal lump of butter; in a cream soup; oven-baked with herb dressing and grated cheese; or marinated in mint vinegar (*see* p. 85), and added to a green salad. However you plan to serve them, they should first be boiled in two waters.

## Pickled Fiddleheads

Remove all bits of brown husk from the fiddleheads by rubbing them in your hands, or by tossing them about in a paper bag. Cook them in boiling water for 5 minutes. Drain. Add clean boiling water and cook them for 5 minutes more. Drain thoroughly, and pack in sterilized jars.

Fill up each jar with this scalding hot mixture, boiled for 5 minutes:

    2 tbsp. sugar
    1 tsp. salt
    1 tsp. celery seed
    1 tsp. tarragon
    1/2 cup water
    1-1/2 cups vinegar.

Seal and store for a month, at least, before serving.

# (Scented) Geranium

There are many varieties of this cultivated plant; but perhaps the most popular is the rose-scented geranium. Generations of Canadian cooks have used its fragrant leaves to ·lend a distinctive flavour to their apple jelly.

If none of your friends grow this plant, try the florist.

### Rose Geranium Jelly

1 cup strawberry juice
2-1/2 cups clear, pure apple juice
1/2 cup lemon juice, strained
1 pkg. pectin crystals
stems from 8 geranium leaves

Bring to a full boil, stirring. Add 4 cups sugar and boil for 1 minute. Remove the stems. Pour into sterilized jars with a rose geranium leaf in each jar. Seal with parowax.

It is possible to make this jelly at any time of the year, using pure apple juice (canned, if you wish), and the juice from frozen strawberries.

# Wild Ginger

One of the first spring plants to carpet the woods, in our area, is the wild ginger, with its two large heart-shaped leaves, and its three-petaled, maroon-coloured blossom, almost at ground level. Even in the richest soil, the plant seldom grows higher than eight or ten inches. The root is easily gathered, for it runs along just under the surface of the soil. It has the distinct smell and taste of ginger, although not as strong as the commercial product. Because we like a stronger flavour, we add ground ginger, whenever we make use of the wild plants.

In earlier times, the root was dried, and grated for use as a seasoning, or brewed as tea for the treatment of indigestion and flatulence. Fresh, it combines with grapefruit and lemon in a tangy marmalade, and with rhubarb, or with green apples, for jam. With the price of preserved ginger soaring, we are happy to make use of this substitute, which nature offers so freely in our area. Although I have found time and patience for the process only once, ginger root can be pre-cooked, peeled, and simmered in a rich syrup to produce preserved ginger.

## Wild Ginger and Rhubarb Jam

Scrub all soil from the ginger roots.
Cut into 1 inch lengths, to make
2 cups root, and simmer,
covered, in 2 cups water, until the root is tender (about 10 minutes).
Cool. Strain the liquid over
4 cups chopped rhubarb,
2 lemons, juice and grated peel,
in the jam kettle.
Peel the root, just lifting off the
gauze-like outer skin.
Cut each piece in two and add to the rhubarb.
Stir in 4 cups sugar.
Bring to the boil, and cook gently for
20 minutes, stirring frequently.
Add 1 tbsp. butter and 2 tsp. ground ginger,
and boil 1 minute more.
Bottle, and seal with parowax.

# Goldenrod

Goldenrod needs no introduction; for surely every corner of Canada abounds in at least one of the more than fifty varieties of this tall, wild plant with its feathery foliage and bright yellow bloom. None is poisonous. Look for it in late summer and early autumn. The Sweet Goldenrod, with its faint licorice flavour, was steeped to a medicinal tea by Indian herbalists. And a friend tells me that any goldenrod bloom, crushed or chopped, adds a little something extra to your best soup recipe. I cannot speak from experience on that subject; but I can of goldenrod wine. It is little trouble to make, and the finished product is delicate and golden, pleasing both the palate and the eye. I have discovered it to be one wine that definitely improves with age. No matter how great the temptation, do not drink it before two years.

## Goldenrod Wine

3 lbs. sugar
1 gal. water
6 large heads goldenrod bloom [Use only the yellow parts.]
1/2 lb. raisins
2 oranges, sliced paper-thin
2 lemons, sliced paper-thin
yeast

Boil sugar and water together 3 minutes. Add the flowers, raisins and fruit, and simmer for 5 minutes.

Turn into a crock, cool to lukewarm, and add yeast. Let it stand in a warm place, covered, for 10 days, stirring daily.

Strain into fermentation jar and let it work for 2 months, or until perfectly clear. Bottle and store.

# Gooseberry

The wild gooseberry bush grows in pastures and along fences. The fruit is not pleasant to pick, for most of the small round berries are covered with the sharp little prickles that early earned it the name of *thornberry*. But it's worth the effort, especially since cultivated gooseberries have become increasingly difficult to locate on summer markets. Because of its prickles, the wild berry is not as suitable for jam or preserve as for wine and jelly.

All cultivated varieties have smooth fruit.

## Ripe Gooseberry Jelly

Simmer 3 qts. wild or cultivated ripe gooseberries (turned to dull-red in colour), in 3 cups water until they are soft.
Strain through cloth, to yield
4-1/2 cups gooseberry juice.
Stir in 1 pkg. pectin crystals and bring to a full boil. Add 5 cups sugar and boil for 1 minute.
Bottle, and seal with parowax.

## The Ettrick Jam

At a craft fair several years ago, one of the exhibitors gave me this recipe from one of her cookbooks, dated 1847. The jam is tart and rich.

3  lbs. large, smooth green gooseberries
3  lemons, juice and peel
3  lbs. sugar

Combine the ingredients in the jam kettle and let sit overnight.

Next day, heat slowly to the boil, stirring constantly, then let it cook rapidly until it tests for set.

## Spiced Gooseberries

Thirty years ago, the Co-operative Commonwealth Federation (CCF) Party authorized publication of a cookbook titled *Canadian Favourites* – "Compiled by a committee of CCF women from favourite recipes submitted by house-wives across the country." However deeply political loyalties may differ, there seems to be unanimous appreciation of this cookbook. In the years since the book's publication several of these favourites from widely different localities and nationalities have been incorporated into our family's recipe files. Our Oatmeal Macaroons are by Mrs. Syms of Nipawin, Saskatchewan. Belgian Waffles, our yeast pancake batter, is from Mrs. DeJeet of Reserve Mines, Cape Breton. And, from Saint John, N.B., one of the most prized, B. M. Horncastle's recipe for Spiced Gooseberries.

2 qts. smooth gooseberries
3 cups brown sugar
1/2 cup malt vinegar
1/2 tsp. cloves
1 tsp. cinnamon

Cook until thick.

Delicious with cold roast beef, or spread on one slice of a bread-and-cheese sandwich.

# Grape

To write of the grape is to write of antiquity. The making of wine from grapes is an ancient art, one which is woven into the fabric of many European and Asian cultures – into their song, painting and sculpture, their social life, as well as into their economy. The *Oxford Book of Food Plants* estimates that grapes have been under cultivation for some six thousand years.

Like the small wild apple, the wild grape is native to Canada. There are two distinct varieties: one deep-purple when ripe, the other with a kind of rich blue bloom. All are too sour to be palatable as fresh fruit; but they make delicious jelly, catsup, wine and juice. Leaves, as well as fruit, are edible. Many old recipes make use of grape leaves in crock pickle and in cooking wild game. And a fresh, delicate wine can be made in early summer, whenever the young grape leaves are fully formed. This is a dry, light wine:

### Grape Leaf Wine

3 lbs. young grape leaves, wild or cultivated
1 gal. boiling water
2 lbs. sugar
yeast

Pour the boiling water over the grape leaves in a crock. Cover with a towel and let stand 5 days, squeezing the leaves thoroughly each day.

Strain off the liquid. Heat it, and dissolve the sugar in it.

Cool to lukewarm and add the yeast.

Set away to work for 3 or 4 months. Bottle, and store it for a couple of years.

### Wild Grape Juice

Serve half-in-half with water, soda water, or ginger ale.

4 qts. wild grapes, stripped from the stems
3 qts. water

Cover the grapes with the water, in the preserving kettle. Simmer for 25 minutes, bruising them with a wooden spoon frequently.
Strain off the juice.
For each cup of juice, allow 1/2 cup sugar.
Boil for 5 minutes.
Bottle in sterilized jars or bottles.

## Lady Flavelle's Grape Catsup

The next recipe is from the *Wimodausis Club Cook Book* – which I wish I were fortunate enough to own. The Wimodausis Club was a small group of Toronto ladies who organized themselves, in 1906, to do social service work wherever help was needed throughout the city. The name of the organization was taken from the first syllables of the words wives, mothers, daughters and sisters. Perhaps their most significant contribution was to the Earlscourt Children's Home. Funds to help operate the Home were raised through sales of their cookbook. A friend loaned me a copy of the third edition, published forty years ago. It contains nearly two thousand recipes, each one complete with the name of its contributor.

4  lbs. grapes
1-1/2  lbs. sugar
1  tsp. salt
1  pint vinegar
1  tsp. each ground cloves, cinnamon and black
    pepper

Stew grapes and strain. Add other ingredients and boil until it thickens. [*Note:* The word "strain" may not be accurate enough for one who has not cooked with grapes previously. The juice will strain through. Then, using a wooden spoon, force the pulp through the sieve or colander, until little but the actual seeds remain.]

Grape Catsup is delicious with a roast of venison, if ever you are lucky enough to have a roast of venison. Meanwhile, serve it with roast beef.

## Grape Conserve

6  cups red or blue Canadian grapes
2  cups chopped ripe pears
1  orange, juice and grated peel
1/2  cup lemon juice
5  cups sugar
1  cup broken pecans

Separate the skins of the grapes from the pulp.
   Simmer the pulp for 10 minutes, then sieve it to eliminate seeds. Add this puree to the skins, in the preserving kettle, then stir in all other ingredients except the nuts. Boil gently until thick. Add pecans. Bottle, and seal with parowax.

# Hawthorn

The hawthorn may well be a relative of the native wild apple; for the shape and formation of the red haw is similar to a tiny crab-apple. Its tenacious growth – in rocky pastures, along lanes and footpaths, in river flats where the chokecherries and wild grapes cluster – has increased the number of its family members throughout Canada to well over one hundred. They range in size from four-foot shrubs to gnarled trees, and almost all have wicked-looking thorns on their branches. The fruit, which ripens from early to late autumn, varies in size from that of a chokecherry to a small crab, and in colour from lemon-yellow to deep crimson.

Often the haws are too wormy for use. But one can usually find a few trees with firm, good fruit. It can be made into a wine so alive and exuberant that it is a good idea to check the corks, from time to time, during its months of maturing. Hawthorn Jelly has a unique flavour, reminiscent of rose petal and quince. And Hawthorn Syrup is a pleasant addition to fruit punch. In making each of these, the haws are covered with water and boiled until they are soft, gray, and muddy-looking. Then they are strained, and lemon juice added to the liquid. Immediately, all the colour is restored; and your wine, or syrup, or jelly, will be a lovely clear red.

In May, the hawthorn tree is a mass of pure-white bloom having a sharp, distinctive fragrance suggestive of wild plum blossom. Hawthorn flowers have long been used to flavour mead; and several early cookbooks combine hawthorn flowers with early rhubarb to make a wine called

## Mid May Wine

1 qt. hawthorn blossom
2 qts. rhubarb, chopped fine
1 cup raisins
1 gal. water
2-1/2 lbs. sugar
yeast

Boil the water and sugar together for 3 minutes and pour over the first 3 ingredients, in a crock. Cool to lukewarm and add the yeast. Cover with a thick towel, and leave in a warm place for 10 days, stirring and bruising the fruit and blossom daily.

Strain. Set the fermentation jar in a cool place, to work for 3 months, then bottle if it is perfectly clear.

This wine matures slowly.

Hawthorn (flower)

## Hawthorn Mead

4 qts. red hawthorn berries
1 gal. water
3/4 cup lemon juice
2-1/2 lbs. liquid honey
yeast

Wash the haws, and boil them in the water until they are soft enough to bruise with a wooden spoon. Strain off the muddy-looking liquid into a crock. Add the lemon juice to it, and it will turn a delicate, deep-pink shade. Stir in 2 lbs. of the honey, dissolving it completely.

Cool to lukewarm, and add the yeast. Set the covered crock in a warm place for 2 weeks.

Stir in the remaining 1/2 lb. honey, then strain the liquor into a fermentation jar and set away to work for 3 or 4 months, at which time it should be still and clear and ready to bottle. But do not drive the corks in tightly for another month or so.

## Hawthorn Jelly

Hawthorn Jelly belongs with toasted English muffins.

Just cover 4 qts. haws with water, and boil until soft.

Crush them – or use the blender – and strain the juice through cloth, to yield 5-1/2 cups. It will be a muddy-looking liquid. Add 1/2 cup strained lemon juice, and the liquid will turn a delicate red. Stir in 1 pkg. pectin crystals and bring to a full boil. Add 6 cups sugar, and boil for 1 minute.

## Hedgerow Jelly

Our first batch of Hedgerow Jelly resulted from an October hike, when miles of rambling yielded only an assortment of wild fruits – not enough of any one kind to be useful. The combined jelly was so delicious that I have made it many times since, deliberately.

2 cups hawthorn juice
1 cup rowanberry juice
1 cup rose hip juice
2 cups wild apple juice
1/2 cup strained lemon juice
1 pkg. pectin crystals

Bring to a full boil.
Add 6-1/2 cups sugar and boil until it tests for set.

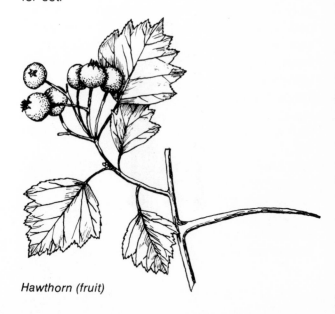

*Hawthorn (fruit)*

# Horseradish

## Horseradish Jelly

Serve with cheese and biscuits, meat, or fish.

1  8-oz. jar horseradish (do not use a brand with
   cream added)
1  tsp. grated sweet red pepper
1/2  cup vinegar
3  cups canned apple juice
1  pkg. pectin crystals

Bring all to the boil, and add

4  cups sugar.

Boil 1 minute. Before bottling, let it sit in the kettle
for 15 minutes, so that the grated ingredients will
be evenly distributed rather than gathered at the
top of each jar.

# *Maple*

No collection of Canadian preserves could be complete without mention of the maple tree. It was not by chance that a patriotic poet used the image of *The Maple Leaf Forever.* The rhythm of the lyrics would have been equally unbroken if the word had been basswood or poplar or chestnut or any of several other trees that filled the forests of this new land. But from the beginning, the maple held a singularly important place in the lives of the settlers. In their wilderness clearings, where both the price and availability of imported sugar were prohibitive, the maple tree was wealth.

From the sap that flowed from the dark trunks in the first bright days of early spring, the settlers instituted the art of Canadian preserving. They brewed maple beer, reminiscent of the refreshing molasses ale made in the cottage kitchens of their homeland. They made kegs of maple vinegar, crocks of wine, and enough syrup and sugar to provide the year's supply of sweetening. With it, wild fruits were made into preserves and jam; and, after the land had been cleared for gardens, cucumbers and melons and other vegetables were pickled in crocks of maple vinegar, for winter use. How bleak would have been their fare without the maple.

Early Canadian documents are rich with references to the value of this tree in the daily lives of our forefathers; but perhaps none is more interesting than this extract from a letter published in Dublin in 1833, in *Letters From Upper Canada.* The writer is a servant girl named Briget Lacey, whose master bought four hundred acres of land in the Huron Tract in Upper Canada. In December, 1832, Briget was reporting back to her friend Mary

Thompson in Ireland, her impressions of life in the Canadian wilderness:

> What flogged all that I had ever seen, was making sugar out of a tree, Mary – not a word of a lie do I tell you; you take a big gimlet and make a hole in the tree, (the maypole, I think they call it) and out comes the shuggar, like sweet water, and you boil it . . . but there's one tree I'm sure of and that's a plumb tree, wild in the woods, for I pull'd with my own hands more than I could eat and carry away, and we boiled them with the maypole shuggar, and a fine parcel of jam we had, all for nothing but our trouble.

Today, due to intricate economic, geographic and social factors, the production of maple products is largely a subject for nostalgia. Millions of Canadians have never seen a sugar shanty nor a "boiling"; and pure maple syrup has become a luxury many cannot afford. But, when I was a child, my family was fortunate to spend unforgettable vacations at my father's boyhood home in Leeds County. There were still large stands of sugar maples in that part of Ontario; and, while not dependent on the sweet as the pioneers had been, maple syrup and sugar were part of the year 'round daily diet of the area residents. What luxury it was – to a town child – that bowl of steaming hot oatmeal with golden maple syrup instead of sugar and milk. My Uncle Art would hurry in from the hayfield to attack the green-apple pie, still warm from the oven; he'd pour maple syrup over it from the jug that was always on the table, and smack his lips at us in loud appreciation. There was also maple syrup pie with meringue on top, and my Aunt Ethel's white cake with maple icing. But best of all were the slices of hot toast, dripping with melted butter, and smothered with maple shavings, which we carved from the big sugar block on the shelf in the pantry.

Whenever our Easter holiday visit coincided with sugar-making, we spent a week of sheer joy. The sugar shanty was a world apart. It was like no building we'd ever been in, no world we'd ever known; and for one week we haunted it day and night, while the laws of ordinary living were all but suspended. We plodded through over-the-boot-tops slush and snow to help gather the sap, and never caught cold. We ate whenever we wanted food – thick wedges of bread spread with the dairy butter my brothers loathed and I loved, and fresh eggs my Aunt Ethel gathered on her way to the sugar shanty and cooked in the boiling sap whenever a child looked either cold or hungry. There were brews of strong green tea sweetened with the hot syrup. Sometimes, surfeited with warmth and food and wonder, we'd curl up on the big woodpile in the corner and doze off – but never for long, lest we miss the next gathering of sap. Hours later than bedtime, we'd lean close against my comfortable aunt in the mysterious, lantern-lighted shanty where we waited to "finish off", and listen to her wry, wise estimates of neighbourhood characters and events. We all, children and grown-ups, stumbled from exhaustion as we made our way back to the house in the middle of the night; but to one child, at least, it was a treasure never lost.

I have written at such length about maple be-cause it is of a day that is fast vanishing. For the same reason – this 1846 recipe for

## Maple Beer

To a gallon of water, add a pint of dark heavy maple syrup, a teaspoon of spruce essence, and some yeast. Ready to drink in 3 days. [In place of the spruce essence, try it with 2 tbsp. lemon juice and 1 cup fresh-made tea.]

## Maple-Cider Wine

3 qts. fresh apple cider
1 pt. maple syrup
yeast

Heat the syrup to lukewarm and stir it into the cider, in a crock, until thoroughly mixed.

Sprinkle in the yeast, and cover the crock with a heavy towel. Keep it in a warm place for 2 weeks, stirring daily. Strain into a fermentation jar, and set away in a cool place to work quietly for 3 or 4 months. Bottle when it is perfectly clear and still.

# *Sweet Marjoram*

This herb is a hardy annual. Start the seeds in-doors, then transplant in late May. From mid-July until the heaviest frost you will have fresh marjoram for omelettes, soups, fish casseroles, and herb vinegar. Just before the first real snow-fall, bring in what remains, and dry it for all-winter use.

## Marjoram Vinegar

1 pt. marjoram leaves and stems
1 qt. vinegar

Pour the vinegar over the marjoram foliage in a glass or plastic container with a tight-fitting cover. Each day for 3 days, bruise the leaves with a wooden spoon. Strain off the vinegar, through cloth, until not a drop of moisture is left. Bottle and cork.

Mix Marjoram Vinegar with melted butter and spoon it over baking fish. Use it as a base for salad dressings, and to marinate cucumber and onion and anything else you like marinated.

## Sweet Marjoram Jelly

Sweet Marjoram Jelly can be made from the dried leaves. But like all herb jellies, it has a fresher flavour when made from the green foliage.

2 cups fresh-picked marjoram
2-1/2 cups water

Follow the directions in recipe for Bee Balm Jelly (on page 36). Before sealing with parowax, set a small sprig of marjoram in the top of each jar.

# *Marrow*

The rather colourless squash-like marrow was never very appealing to me as a vegetable, even when oven-baked and basted liberally with lemon butter and chopped cress. But since being educated in its uses by a friend who grows it each summer I have discovered it has all sorts of culinary possibilities. We unearthed a recipe for a delicious jam of marrow and dried apricots; another for marrow, pineapple and lemon; marrow pickle; marrow and green pepper chutney; and this confection known as

## Marrow Cream

Boil 4 lbs. marrow until tender. Drain thoroughly. Using the electric beater, as for whipped potatoes, beat the marrow with:

  1/2 lb. butter
  the grated peel and the juice of 4 lemons

Stir in 3 lbs. sugar, and boil for 20 minutes, stirring all the time.

Marrow Cream may be used for a filling between cake layers, or in tart shells, as well as a jam.

# *Mayapple*

One of the loveliest flowers to be found in the woods in late spring is the Mayapple. It grows in extravagant clumps in the moist forest soil, or in well-shaded fence corners and roadsides; and the plants are recognizable from a distance by their large, umbrella-like leaves, which give it a lush, tropical look. Each plant's single flower is like a waxy white rose with a golden centre; and it is tucked underneath the leaf canopy, close to the stem. The bloom has a musky fragrance, not unpleasant, but a bit overpowering. Throughout the summer, the blossom changes to an egg-shaped green "apple", with a shiny outer skin; and as the fruit ripens to yellow by mid-August, it is plain to see why the plant has also been known as the *Wild Lemon*.

The Mayapple is a relative of the Mediterranean Mandrake family. For centuries its root has been valued for medicinal purposes; but when friendly Indians instructed the first settlers in its use, they were careful to warn them that, taken in any quantity, the root is poisonous. Some herbalists claim that the leaves, too, may be deadly. But there is no doubt about the fruit. It produces marmalade, jam, jelly, preserve and juice that are unique in flavour – faintly resembling cantaloup or ground cherry, yet with something that is peculiarly Mayapple.

Gather the fruit before it is soft and overripe. It should be firm, and just turned pale yellow, with even a touch of the cool green colour still showing. Even then the pulp has a bland taste, and requires a citrus fruit to sharpen it. Overripe, it is decidedly flat.

## Mayapple Jam

2-1/2 qts. Mayapples
1-1/2 cups water

Remove stem and blossom ends, and quarter the fruit. Simmer in the water until completely soft, then force it through a colander or sieve to remove all seeds. Take:

4 cups Mayapple puree
3 limes, or 3 lemons, quartered, and sliced paper-thin
1 pkg. pectin crystals

Bring slowly to a full boil, stirring frequently. Add 4 cups sugar and boil hard for 1 minute. Before bottling stir in 2 tsp. ground ginger.

## Mayapple Juice

Remove the stem and blossom ends from 3 qts. Mayapples. Add 1 qt. water. Cover, and simmer until the fruit is soft. Crush with a wooden spoon, or mallet, and simmer for 5 minutes more. Strain through a plastic sieve, letting it sit until the pulp is completely dry. Then strain the juice through cloth.

This juice will keep, refrigerated, for 2 or 3 weeks. Add it to orange juice, or lemonade, or to any white wine.

### *Mayapple Syrup*

Boiled for 5 minutes, with 1/4 cup sugar to each cup of juice, it can be bottled for winter use.

### *Mayapple Jelly*

Allowing 3-1/2 cups Mayapple juice and 1/2 cup lemon juice to 1 pkg. pectin crystals and 4-1/2 cups sugar, yields a jelly that more than makes up in flavour what it lacks in colour.

# *Melon*

The original melon was a tropical plant, native to Africa. But throughout the centuries it has adapted itself to many differing climates and soils, and some varieties grow successfully in a temperate climate. Early settlers from Britain found that because of the long, hot Canadian summers, melons grew better here than they did back home.

While melon is commonly eaten as a raw fruit, delicious wine, preserve, pickle and conserve can be made from all members of this luxuriant family.

## Cantaloup Conserve

6 cups diced cantaloup, not too ripe
2 cups diced pears
3 lemons, grated peel and juice
1 doz. maraschino cherries, halved
5 cups sugar
1/2 cup slivered almonds

Bring first 5 ingredients slowly to the boil, stirring to prevent sticking to the bottom of the kettle. Cook gently until thick. Stir in almonds, then remove from heat. Bottle, and seal with parowax.

## Melon Chutney

2 qts. prepared melon rind
1 qt. cold water
salt
3 sweet red peppers
3 green peppers
1 small hot red pepper
2 lemons
2 Spanish onions
1 qt. cider vinegar
2 cups brown sugar
2 tsp. each mace, cinnamon, dry mustard, paprika
2 tbsp. each curry powder, ginger and celery seed

Remove outer rind and soft inner portions from melon rind. Chop coarsely, and soak in water and 3 tbsp. salt, overnight.

Chop fine the peppers, onions, and lemons, sprinkle them with 1/2 cup salt and let stand overnight.

Next day, rinse and drain the rind. Drain the other vegetables and mix with the chopped rind in the preserving kettle. Add the other ingredients; bring to the boil and cook gently for 45 minutes. Seal in hot sterilized jars.

## Rosy Watermelon Pickle

This recipe is from the *Historical Sketch and Cook Book* compiled about twenty-five years ago by the Woman's Auxiliary of Holy Trinity Church, Little Current, Ontario, on Manitoulin Island. I have never tasted better pickled melon.

2 lbs. watermelon rind
1 qt. water
1/2 cup maraschino cherries
2 cups sugar
1-1/2 cups light corn syrup
1-1/2 cups vinegar
1 tsp. salt
1 lemon, thinly sliced
2 tbsp. cinnamon bark
1 tbsp. whole cloves

Trim dark green and pink parts off rind, cut rind in 1 inch cubes. Cover with water. [I add 1 tsp. powdered alum.] Simmer until tender, about 15 minutes. Drain thoroughly. Combine cherries, sugar, syrup, vinegar and salt. Tie lemon and spices in a bag. Simmer all until rind is clear, about 40 minutes. Seal in hot sterile jars. Makes 2 pints.

# *Mint*

The Mint family, both cultivated and wild, is a large one, with many subtle variations in both flavour and fragrance. But, however the varieties may differ, they all taste and smell cool, green and minty.

Mint, like the grape, is rooted in folklore and myth. To the ancient Greeks it was the symbol of wisdom, as well as a medicine, perfume, food, and air freshener. The Indians dried the leaves and used them in winter; and the early settlers followed their example and were glad to have this substitute for China tea.

Recipes for minted drinks are numerous – wines, cordials, shrubs, liqueurs, juleps. One of the rare old ones is this

## Brandy Smash

2 qts. best brandy
1 lb. sugar brought to boil in
1 qt. water.
Peel in spirals 12 small lemons

Pour the brandy over the lemon peel, and 1 cup fine-chopped fresh mint, then add the boiling syrup. Cool. Serve in glasses with chopped ice and a sprig of fresh mint.

## Mint Vinegar

1 cup brown sugar
1 qt. cider vinegar
2 cups washed mint leaves

Bring sugar and vinegar to the boil and add the mint leaves. Crushing the leaves against the side of the kettle with a spoon, bring it back to the boil and let it simmer gently for 5 minutes. Strain, and bottle in sterile bottles, well-corked.

Mix Mint Vinegar with oil, salt, and fresh-ground pepper for a tangy salad-dressing. Or marinate orange and avocado slices in it, then serve them on a bed of lettuce and chopped parsley.

## Mint Chutney
## (uncooked)

12  ripe tomatoes, peeled
 6  tart apples, peeled and cored
 1  cup raisins
 2  sweet red peppers
 1  small hot red pepper
 4  large onions
 3  cups brown sugar
 1  tbsp. salt
 2  tbsp. celery seed
 1  tbsp. dry mustard
 1  tbsp. ground ginger
 3  cups fresh-gathered mint leaves
 4  cups cider vinegar

Bring vinegar, sugar, salt and spices to the boil for 1 minute, then pour it over all the other ingredients, which have either been chopped very fine or done in the blender. (The blender method is so easy.) Cover the crock with a thick towel, and let it stand, covered, for 2 weeks, stirring it once each day. Heat to the boil, bottle, and seal.

## Kaye White's Champagne Jelly

3-1/2  cups hard cider
1/2  cup lemon juice
a cupful of fresh mint leaves

Heat together slowly until it comes to the boil. Cover it, and let it stand for 3 minutes, then strain it to remove the mint leaves. Put the liquid into the jelly kettle, with 1 pkg. pectin crystals; and when it comes to the boil, add:

4  cups sugar.

Boil 1 minute. Bottle, and seal with parowax.

## Minted Green Grape Jelly

Gather 2 qts. grapes, either wild or cultivated, while they are still hard and green, but full-formed. Simmer them for 20 minutes, in a kettle with 4 cups water and a generous handful of fresh-picked mint leaves, crushing frequently, as they soften, with a wooden spoon. Strain through a sieve, and then through cloth, to obtain 4 cups juice.
Add 2 or 3 drops green vegetable colouring and a pkg. pectin crystals and bring to the boil.
Stir in 4-1/2 cups sugar, and boil until it tests for set. Bottle. When cool, set a fresh mint leaf in the top of each jar, and seal with parowax.

# *Mulberry*

The word *mulberry* sounds slightly exotic to me; for it recalls an afternoon, long ago, when our grade-four teacher first told us the magical tale of tiny worms spinning fragile silken threads on mulberry shrubs in Chinese gardens. No one in our neighbourhood had a mulberry tree, and it was some time before I realized that mulberries aren't only for silkworms. They are a delicious, juicy fruit, resembling thimbleberries (p. 39), but smaller and more delicate in flavour.

Sometimes the ornamental mulberry is actually a bush – remember the mulberry bush of the "Here we go round" chant. But it may also grow to be a tall tree with spreading branches. The berries start to ripen in mid-summer and continue on into September, turning first rosy-red, then almost black. Unless the fruit is picked before it is dead-ripe, the grass, garden, and lawn furniture will be littered with wine-dark berries.

Newcomers to Upper and Lower Canada brought cuttings of this tree from their English gardens, where it had grown for centuries. Since it is not native, and at first survived the severe Canadian winters only with difficulty, it has not proliferated in this country. We spotted one, many summers ago, in an abandoned farm garden; now season after season, both the birds and ourselves harvest mulberries throughout the month of August. They can be made into mulberry pie, with a half-cupful of pitted sour cherries added to sharpen the flavour of the mulberries; mulberry jam and jelly; and mulberry wine. Many of the old wine recipes tell us to simmer the fruit; but since the flavour of mulberries is so difficult to retain, I prefer this method:

## Mulberry Wine

Boil together for 5 minutes 1 gal. water, 2 lbs. sugar, and 3 lemons sliced very thin. Pour this over 3 qts. mulberries which have been crushed in a crock. Cool to lukewarm and add yeast. Stir daily for a week, then strain through cloth. Let it work in a fermentation jar until it is still and clear, then siphon it off and bottle it.

## Mulberry Butter

2 qts. mulberries
6 tart green apples

Proceed as for Wild Blackberry Butter (p. 38).

## Mulberry Jelly

2 qts. mulberries, not too dead-ripe
2 cups water.
Simmer together until the juice runs freely and the
berries are soft, crushing frequently with a
wooden spoon, as they cook.
Strain the juice through cloth to measure
3 cups mulberry juice. Add
1 cup dry red wine
1 pkg. pectin crystals.
Bring to the boil, and stir in
4-1/2 cups sugar.
Boil for 1 minute. Bottle, and seal with parowax.

# *Mushroom*

My gastronomic preoccupation with the mushroom dates back many years, to an autumn I once spent with friends in a lonely farmhouse on an island in the St. Lawrence River. Throughout that golden September and October we ate mushrooms, which to me had always been a luxury item, as if they were as common as bread and milk. Even breakfast included fresh-picked mushrooms fried in butter and heaped on a thick slice of home-made bread toasted over the wood coals. At other times – mushrooms floating whole and succulent in the brown gravy, or an unforgettable supper casserole of mushrooms in whipped potato and herbed sour cream.

As we gathered mushrooms on those September afternoons, I became fascinated by this gift of nature, about which I knew so little. My hostess knew a lot about them; she impressed upon me the danger of eating just any mushroom. To this day, unless the mushrooms are from the store, I check them in the book before cooking.

When you are out hiking in the fall, don't overlook that aristocrat of the mushroom family, the puff-ball. There are two kinds, one edible and one non-edible, even of these. The edible puff-ball is white all through when sliced. Marinate the half-inch-thick slices in sauterne for a couple of hours, then *sauté* them gently in butter until golden-brown, and you'll wish you could find a puff-ball every day of the week.

Mushroom Ketchup is delicious with cold meat. Many of the old recipes for this condiment are involved and time-consuming. Most remarkable is the one included in Canada's first cookbook, *The Cook Not Mad; or Rational Cookery,* published in Kingston in 1831. (There are only two copies of it known to be in existence now, but recently a partial reprint has appeared.) The recipe in the original calls for mushrooms, minced anchovies, spices, and strong ale; and it promises "an excellent ketchup which will keep good more than twenty years."

### Mushroom Ketchup (Modern method)

2 lbs. mushrooms
1 small onion
1 cup wine vinegar

Whirl all in the blender till smooth. Put in a saucepan with 2 tsp. salt, 1 tsp. black pepper, 2 tbsp. sugar, and 2 tbsp. pickling spice tied in muslin. Simmer gently for 1/2 hr., stirring frequently. Remove spice bag. Bottle and seal.

## Pickled Mushrooms

An 1861 *Canadian Housewife's Manual of Cookery* offers this "excellent way to pickle mushrooms to preserve the flavour":

Buttons must be rubbed with a bit of flannel and salt. Throw a little salt over, and put them into a stew-pan with some mace and pepper. As the liquor comes out, shake them well, and keep them over a gentle fire till all of it be dried into them again; then put as much vinegar into the pan as will cover them, give it one warm, and turn all into a glass or stone jar. They will keep 2 years and are delicious.

## Pickled Mushrooms (Modern Style)

This recipe is more trouble than the one above; but it, too, is delicious.

Choose choice small firm mushrooms. Wipe each one with a soft cloth, and leave them in a bowl, overnight, sprinkled with salt. Next day, put them in a saucepan over low heat until the juice evaporates, shaking the pan constantly to keep them from sticking. Do not boil them or they will go soft. Remove from heat and pack in small sterilized jars. Fill up each jar with a scalded, then cooled, mixture of the following:

  white wine vinegar
  fresh ground black pepper
  ground mace
  chopped fresh thyme leaves.

If you gather your own mushrooms, you too will be interested in this item from the *Canadian Housewife's Manual of Cookery:*

> Preparing a supper dish of Puree of Mushrooms. Throw in with them a small onion to test their goodness, as, if there is a bad or poisonous one among them, the onion will turn of a bluish-black while cooking. In that case, throw them all away.

However, I would not rely on any simple test to distinguish between edible and poisonous mushrooms. (See p. 132 for suggested guides.)

# *Wild Onion*

Almost before the snow is out of the swamp each spring, clumps of new-green, grass-like shoots announce the return of the wild onion. We use a trowel to dig up the small white bulbs; then we sprinkle white and green parts both with salt, wrap a slice of bread and butter around a handful of them – and are certain that no garden onion could taste quite so good.

The Indians used them to flavour their pemmican, a mixture of dried meat or fish and bear or goose grease. We add wild onions to stew, salad, and potato cream soup. And each April we make the year's supply of

## Wild Onion Jelly

1  cup coarsely chopped wild onion, bulbs and . some of the greens
1  cup water
1/2  cup cider vinegar
2  cups apple juice
1/2  tsp. salt
fresh-ground black pepper
1  pkg. pectin crystals

Bring all to a full boil, and stir in

3-1/2  cups sugar.

Boil for 1 minute, or until it tests for set. Do not bottle it for 15 or 20 minutes, so that the chopped onion will be distributed evenly, rather than settling at the top of each jar.

Serve Wild Onion Jelly with cheese and biscuits, or omelette, or with the season's first pan-fried trout.

## Red Onion Relish

Chop fine (I use the blender for this):

6  large red onions
2  large sweet red peppers
1  small hot red pepper

Sprinkle with 1/2 cup salt. Add 2 cups ice-cold water and let sit in a bowl overnight. Next day, drain it thoroughly. Boil together for 3 minutes:

1  cup vinegar
3/4  cup sugar
2  tbsp. pickling spice tied loosely in cloth.

Add the onions and peppers and heat to the boil again. Remove the spice bag. Add 1/2 cup dry red wine. Bottle and seal.

# *Parsley*

As I write, I am reminded of a day when a young mother and her five-year-old joined us for afternoon tea. As the platter of sandwiches circulated, I heard her say, "It's parsley dear. Just leave it on the plate. It's only for decoration."

If you use these curly, dark-green clusters for garnishing only, you are missing out on one of the most useful herbs grown. For hundreds of years, herbalists have claimed medicinal value for parsley in treating everything from "low blood" to baldness. And generation after generation of older people have been quite certain that a regular drink of home-made parsley wine is the most effective remedy for rheumatic ills.

If you are a gardener, you will have discovered how simple it is to winter parsley from your garden in a sunny kitchen window. But bunches of it are available the year 'round in most fruit stores, and it can add flavour, as well as food value, to your menus. Try a cream cheese soup with a cupful of chopped parsley and a dash of sherry added just before you take it from the stove; or, for a quick winter lunch, two cups vegetable juice and two chicken bouillon cubes brought to the boil and poured steaming into bowls that contain chopped parsley and a generous lump of butter. Baked fish, with a parsley and lemon butter sauce. A jellied salad, with lime jello, sour cream, chopped parsley, and a dash of onion salt. And there's no sandwich filling more delicious than slices of cucumber and sprigs of parsley marinated for a half-hour in wine vinegar, then drained thoroughly, and sprinkled with salt and fresh-ground pepper.

But on to parsley wine, which has a delicate bouquet and a slightly astringent flavour. Several of the old recipes use ginger; but I omit it, preferring the herb-like flavour unspiced.

## Parsley Wine

4 cups parsley
1 gal. boiling water
2 lemons, sliced thin
2 oranges, sliced thin
3 lbs. sugar
yeast

Pour the boiling water over the parsley and the sliced fruit, in a crock. Bruise well with a wooden spoon, or squeeze with the hands, each day for 3 days. Strain. Warm to lukewarm, and stir in the sugar till all is dissolved, then add the yeast.

Set it away to work in a fermentation jar until it is clear and still. Siphon off, bottle, and store it for at least 6 months.

### Parsley Jelly

4  cups clear apple juice
1/2  cup lime juice
Bring to the boil with
1  pkg. pectin crystals.
Add 4-1/2 cups sugar.
As soon as it tests for set,
add 2 cups chopped
fresh parsley, and remove from heat.
Stir frequently for 15 minutes.
Bottle, and seal with parowax.

### *Variation:*

1  cup grapefruit juice
1/2  cup cider vinegar
2-1/2  cups clear apple juice

Proceed as in the recipe above.

# *Peach*

Although the peach tree is native to the Orient, it has been successfully cultivated in Ontario's Niagara district since the late 1700s. There is no lovelier sight in late spring than a peach orchard in tender pink bloom – unless it is that same orchard, in mid-August, laden with delicately tinted fruit. My childhood was spent far from peach orchards, and the fruit was shipped to us by train. For two or three weeks in late summer we knew all the glamour of feasting on this exotic fruit, which none of us had ever seen except in baskets.

Nothing was wasted. My mother, and all her neighbours, "did down" bushels of peaches in half-gallon jars. There were jars of rich peach preserve, brandied peaches, peach chutney, and a few of peaches pickled whole. Even the peach stones and peelings were put to use: in a jelly made by simmering them for a half-hour in water to cover, then combining the strained juice with an equal quantity of apple juice. Living in a more affluent time, I have not made this jelly; but spread liberally on thick slices of buttered bread, it was a favourite after-school snack.

## Peach Melomel

Use 4 qts. peeled fresh peaches, and follow the directions for Wild Apple Melomel.

## Peach Chutney

12  large, fully ripe peaches, peeled, and chopped coarsely
3  green apples, peeled and chopped
1  large onion, chopped
1  large green pepper, chopped
2  lemons, grated peel and juice

Add all to a syrup made by boiling together for 10 minutes:

3  cups cider vinegar
2  tsp. salt
1  tsp. cayenne
a spice bag with 2 tbsp. mustard seed and 2 tbsp. cassia buds
2  cups dark brown sugar

Simmer for a half-hour. Remove the spice bag. Add 1 tsp. cloves and 2 tsp. ginger and boil gently for 5 minutes more. Bottle and seal.

## Peach and Lemon Jam

This is a smooth "butter", equally good on toast, or in small flaky tart shells with a dot of whipped cream on top.

Using frozen lemonade made up with only 2 tins of water rather than 4, for the required liquid in your blender, make 6 cups of a puree of 2 lemons, unpeeled, and firm ripe peaches, peeled and stoned. To the 6 cups puree, add

    1/4  tsp. salt
    1  tbsp. butter
    1/4  cup lemon juice
    5  cups sugar.

Stir frequently, and boil until it tests for set.

## Peach Preserve

A rich preserve that is definitely party fare. Serve it chilled – but it is better not served at all until it has had a couple of months to mellow.

firm ripe peaches (approx. 4 qts.)
4  lbs. sugar
2  cups water
1  pt. brandy

Boil the sugar and water together 5 minutes. Peel, halve, and stone the peaches, and simmer in the syrup 5 minutes. Remove the halves carefully with a slotted spoon and pack them in pint sealers. Boil the syrup for another 5 minutes, or until thick. Remove from heat and mix in the brandy. Fill up the jars with this, and seal tightly.

## Spiced Peaches

This recipe for pickled peaches goes back to a day when people had to spend many more hours than we do in the simple mechanics of living.

Boil together for 5 minutes:

    4  lbs. sugar
    1  pt. white wine vinegar
    1  tsp. each cloves, allspice, cinnamon, mace, and ginger.

Add 7 lbs. firm ripe peaches, peeled, halved and stoned, and bring slowly to the boil. Remove peach halves gently and pack loosely in quart jars. Fill up the jars with the syrup, saving the extra. Each day for 7 days, pour off all the syrup, heat it to boiling, and pour it back over the peaches in the jars. On the 8th day, boil the syrup for 10 minutes, fill up the jars, and seal tightly. Do not use for 1 month.

# Pear

Pears have been cultivated successfully in Canada since the mid-1700s. Not quite as hardy as the apple, they do, nevertheless, thrive in sheltered orchards; many splendid varieties of the fruit have been developed over the years. By now the tree has gone wild in most areas; and a handful of these hard, sour wild pears added to the more exotic cultivated fruit can lend a sharper, fuller flavour to pear chutney, wine, or conserve.

At one time in England, the fermented juice of pears, *perry,* was as popular a drink as was cider, the fermented juice of apples. But perry was more difficult to produce; for while any old apples, even those in a state of semi-decomposition, can be used for cider, pears are more delicate and perishable, and only the best are suitable for good perry.

Although I have never produced a proper perry, this variation on an old recipe has yielded a wine that is fresh, and slightly effervescent after months in the bottle.

## Pear Mead

6 qts. fully ripe pears.
Wipe them clean with a damp cloth, and remove stems and blossom ends. Quarter a few at a time and crush in a large crock, with a wooden mallet, until all are reduced to a juicy mash.
Pour over them
1 gal. boiling water.
Stir in
1 lb. sugar, and, when cooled to lukewarm, the yeast.
Stir every day for 8 days. Strain through cloth over
2 lbs. liquid clover honey and
1/2 cup strained lemon juice.
When the honey is thoroughly mixed with the juice, put all into a fermentation jar to work for 2 or 3 months.
Pear wine does not clear readily, so you may have to use the white of an egg to fine it.
Store in a cool dark place for at least a year.

The original recipe was for a metheglin – a mixture of fruit juice, honey, and spices. But the flavour of pear is overpowered by that of any spice, so I choose to make it a mead.

## Spiced Pear Butter

8 large, firm ripe pears, unpeeled
2 lemons, juice and peel

If you do not use a blender, boil these together until soft enough to rub through a sieve. (I put the lemon juice, the peel – stripped of the white portion – and the quartered and cored pears in the blender, raw, and it's ready for the kettle in less than a minute.)

To each cup of puree, allow 3/4 cup sugar, and boil until thick, stirring frequently. Add 2 tsp. ginger and 1 tsp. coriander and simmer 3 minutes. Bottle, and seal with parowax.

# Pear Marmalade

(I find either Bartletts, or the later, dark-skinned Bosco pears best for this. They should be firm throughout.)

Simmer in 2 cups water until the liquid is almost evaporated, the grated peel of

   1  grapefruit
   2  lemons
   3  oranges.

Add the juice of these, and 8 cups diced pears, unpeeled. Heat to boiling, and stir in

   6  cups sugar.

Boil gently until thick – between 40 minutes and 1 hour. Just before bottling, stir in a few sliced maraschino cherries, for colour.

# Pear Chutney

1/2  doz. green peppers
2  small hot red peppers
2  large onions
1/4  cup salt

Grind (or chop fine), sprinkle with the salt, and leave covered overnight. Next day, rinse with cold water and drain thoroughly. In a large kettle, simmer for 5 minutes

1  qt. cider vinegar
2  cups brown sugar
1  tbsp. powdered tumeric
1  tsp. celery seed
1  tsp. each ground cloves, allspice and
    mustard.

Stir in the drained vegetables and 4 qts. pears, unpeeled, either coarsely ground or chopped fine. Boil gently for 45 minutes, stirring frequently.

# *Peppers*

Peppers of many varieties – sweet and hot; green, red and yellow – grow successfully in most gardens and bear liberally before the first frost. As well as adding flavour to other vegetable relishes and chutneys, they are delicious pickled by themselves, or in this

## Pepper Relish

6 large green peppers
6 yellow peppers
1 small hot red pepper
6 small onions

Put all through the grinder into a large bowl. Cover with boiling water. Let stand for a half-hour. Drain thoroughly. Simmer for 5 minutes, together:

1 tbsp. salt
1 tbsp. celery seed
1 cup sugar
1-1/2 cups cider vinegar

Add the chopped peppers and onion, bring to the boil, and bottle at once.

## Pepper Jelly

1 cup fine-chopped sweet peppers
1 small hot pepper
1 cup water
1/2 cup cider vinegar
2 cups apple juice
1/2 tsp. salt
1 pkg. pectin crystals

Proceed as for Wild Onion Jelly.

## Pickled Sweet Peppers

Boil together for 2 minutes:

1-1/2 cups vinegar
1/2 tsp. salt
1/2 cup sugar.

Pack whole large red or green sweet peppers in sterilized jars, with a sprig of fresh thyme, or sage, or mint, in each jar. Fill up the jars with the scalding-hot syrup. Seal tightly. Mellow for a month before using.

# *Plum*

The plum tree, like the apple tree, has at least one variety that is native to Canada. The oval-shaped, bright-red, wild plum was manna to the pioneers; and the cuttings brought from France and England, and from settlements in America, for cultivation, could not equal in flavour this native fruit growing so prolifically in every forest clearing.

Today, the wild plum threatens to become extinct. It is less than a dozen years since Sylvia Boorman gathered the title fruit of her delightful *Wild Plums In Brandy;* yet, if she were to search the same localities this autumn, she would be fortunate to harvest even one full basket. If you know of a fence corner, a country lane, where the wild plum still flourishes and bears fruit, mark it well. There is no jelly quite like wild plum jelly.

Plums of many colours, shapes and sizes are cultivated successfully in Canadian orchards; and the fruit has endless possibilities for use. It combines interestingly with other fruits – melon, raspberry, rowanberry, wild apple, blueberry – in jams, jellies and conserves. Old treasured recipes for plum brandy, wine and port are as numerous as the varieties from which they have been brewed – with the small sour damson perhaps heading the list. The colour and bouquet of wild plum wine is in a class by itself – but only a few lucky people will ever taste it.

A rich, port-like wine can be made from any of our blue or purple plums. If you live near an orchard, go and buy them there, near the end of the harvest, when they are fully ripe; and lose as little time as possible between tree and crock.

## Plum Port

6 qts. blue plums, pitted
1/2 cup lemon juice
1 gal. boiling water

Crush the plums – and a half-dozen of the pits – in a crock, with a wooden mallet, until the juice runs freely. Add the lemon juice and water. When lukewarm, add the yeast and 1 lb. sugar.

Cover, and let it stand in a warm place for 2 weeks, stirring it several times each day.

Strain over 2 lbs. sugar in a large vessel, and stir until the sugar is completely dissolved. Transfer it to a fermentation jar and keep it in the same warm place for another 6 weeks. Set the jar away to work for a couple of months until the wine is still and clear. Bottle it, and store it in a cool dark corner for at least a year.

## Plum Catsup

Using 4 lbs. very ripe blue prune plums, proceed as for Grape Catsup.

For added flavour, I boil 1 onion, 1 green pepper, and 1 tsp. crushed chillis with the plums.

## Plum Chutney

Almost twenty years ago, *Chatelaine* magazine published a cookbook of *363 Home-Tested Recipes,* contributed by cooks from every corner of Canada. One of them, Mrs. A. Carmichael of Victoria, B.C., might be pleased to know that at least one reader follows – with a few variations – her recipe for Plum Chutney.

5 lbs. blue plums, cooked, and put through the colander
4 lbs. apples, chopped
3 large onions, chopped
1 tbsp. allspice*, cloves and ginger
salt to taste
4 lbs. brown sugar
1/2 tsp. ground red pepper
3 cups vinegar

Combine plum puree and remaining ingredients. Cook, stirring constantly, until thickened. Seal in sterilized jars.

## Damson Preserve

In *The Cook Not Mad,* published in Kingston in 1831, there is a Damson Preserve that is surely meant only for gifts, and special occasions. It is a sweet, rich, and fragrant blend of tart purple plums and good brandy. Experimenting several times, I have altered method and amounts to arrive, finally, at this much appreciated delicacy.

Boil together for 5 minutes:

3 lbs. sugar
4 cups water.

To this syrup, add 2 oranges, sliced very thin, peel and all, and 3 qts. purple damson plums. Boil together gently for 20 minutes. Remove from heat and add a cupful of good brandy. Bottle and seal. Do not use for a couple of months, as it mellows with time.

*Note:* A cupful of rum can be added instead of the brandy, if you prefer it.

*I use coriander, instead of allspice, in this chutney; and add 1 tsp. dry mustard and 1 tsp. grated horseradish.

## Plum and Cantaloup Jam

The round, blush-pink English plums, which are plentiful on the market in mid-August, combine with ripe cantaloup to make a mellow jam or butter. For a butter, use the blender. For a jam, dice the melon, and stone and quarter the plums.

1 firm ripe cantaloup, peeled and seeded and diced
2 qts. firm ripe plums
grated peel and juice of 2 lemons
3/4 cup sugar for each cup prepared fruit

Simmer all fruit together in the kettle for 5 minutes, then add the sugar. Boil gently until it tests for set – about 20 minutes.

## Minted Green Gage Jelly

3 qts. firm, not-too-ripe green-gage plums, simmered for 15 minutes with
3 cups water and
a handful of fresh mint leaves.
Crush the fruit thoroughly, and strain the juice through cloth. To
5-1/2 cups juice, add
1 pkg. pectin crystals.
Bring to boil, and stir in 6 cups sugar. Boil hard for 1 minute.
Bottle. When the jelly is completely cool, place a fresh mint leaf in the top of each jar,
and seal with parowax.

## Pickled Plums

Choose firm, not-too-ripe plums, any variety, and follow the directions for Spiced Peaches. The small, round pale-yellow plums are especially good for pickling, with a sprig of fresh sage or marjoram leaves in each jar.

## Cardamom Plum Jelly

3 qts. ripe plums – the oval-shaped wild ones, if you're very lucky – or any tart red or dark blue variety, such as damsons
1 pkg. pectin crystals
1 heaped tsp. crushed cardamom seeds
7 cups sugar

Simmer the washed plums in a kettle with 3 cups water, for 20 minutes. Strain the fruit through cloth, to yield

6 cups juice.

Combine plum juice, crushed cardamom seeds and pectin and bring to a full boil. Add the sugar, and boil hard for 1 minute, or until it tests for set. Bottle. Just before sealing with parowax, sprinkle a few grains of cardamom in the top of each jar.

# Pumpkin

The grinning, anything-but-exotic pumpkin is not only for Jack O'Lanterns and pies. It grew in and out among the rows of Indian corn long before the arrival of the first white settlers; and throughout the centuries, as well as being used as feed for farm animals, it has yielded a kind of molasses called Pumpkin Sass, a number of breads, cakes and cookies, a once-popular fruit butter named Pumpkin Honey, a wine (which I have never made nor tasted), and an assortment of conserves, marmalades and chutneys.

## Pumpkin Chutney

(The original old recipe calls for a pumpkin peeled and cleaned out and diced. But you can obtain quite satisfactory results with canned pumpkin.)

4  cups pumpkin
6  large ripe tomatoes, peeled and chopped
2  large onions, chopped fine
2  large peppers, chopped fine
juice and grated peel of 2 lemons
1  cup currants, or chopped raisins
1  tsp. each salt, ground hot red pepper, ginger, cloves, cinnamon and mace
2  cups cider vinegar
1/2  cup dark molasses
2  cups sugar

Boil together gently, stirring frequently, until thick.

Delicious with cream cheese and biscuits.

## Pumpkin Marmalade

4  cups pumpkin, peeled and chopped fine
3  cups chopped pears (Bartletts, if possible)
1  tsp. salt.
Sprinkle 6 cups sugar over it, in a large bowl, and leave overnight.

Next day, add the grated peel and the chopped pulp of
3 oranges and 3 lemons, and put all in the preserving kettle and bring it to the boil very slowly, stirring frequently. Cook until it tests for set, as jam – about 40 minutes.
Bottle, and seal with parowax.

*Note:* There are many variations of the Pumpkin Marmalade recipe. Some use apple sauce instead of the pears. One adds cranberries, another elderberries. And several call for the addition of root ginger.

# *Quince*

Although it dates back to Greek mythology, and the early Romans used it in beauty preparations and perfumes, in our day the quince has become an unfashionable fruit. Perhaps it's because quinces cannot be eaten uncooked; so whoever values this fruit must be prepared to preserve it in some form or other. Whenever we are lucky enough to find a basket of them on a market in late autumn, other shoppers always ask us, "What are those?"

Quinces look like large yellow apples that have become wrinkled and mis-shapen. Bite into one, and you will regret it. But preserved, or in jelly or wine, the flavour is unique – a blend of the refreshing and the exotic. It may be a cultivated taste; you'll probably either love them or not bother with them again.

## Quince Butter

10 large quinces, washed, cored and
    quartered.
Put in the blender with
1 lemon, quartered
3 green apples, quartered and cored
1 cup apple juice.
In the preserving kettle, combine with
3/4 cup sugar for each cup fruit
2 tbsp. butter.
Boil until thick. Just before bottling, add
1/2 cup rum
1 tsp. ground coriander.
Seal with parowax.

## Quince Wine

The 1845 edition of *Modern Practical Cookery* contains a recipe for Quince Wine, which is simple to make and, once tasted, impossible to forget. The method of that day was laborious – all those tough quinces had to be shredded on a grater. I use my blender.

15 large quinces
 1 gal. water
 2 lbs. sugar
yeast

Wipe the quinces clean, and remove the blossom end from each. Quarter them, and put some of them in the blender with a cup of the water, repeating until all the quinces are mashed.

Simmer the fruit for 20 minutes in all the water. Strain. Cool to lukewarm and add yeast. Place in fermentation jar until clear; then bottle. *Note:* This wine takes a longer time than average to mature. Leave it for a year and a half.

If you grow scented geraniums, toss a half-dozen rose geranium leaves into the blender with the quinces. The result will be a mystery to your friends – but a pleasant one.

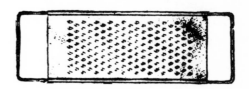

## Quince Conserve

8 large quinces
1/2 cantaloup melon, ripe
2 lemons
1 orange
sugar
12 maraschino cherries.

Wipe clean, remove the blossom end, core, quarter, and dice the quinces. Pare, seed, and dice the cantaloup. Add the grated peel, and juice, of the lemons and oranges. Simmer for 20 minutes. To each cup of the fruit, allow

3/4 cup sugar.

Boil until thick – about 15 minutes – and add the cherries, chopped. Bottle, and seal with parowax.

## Paradise Jelly

3 cups chopped quinces
2 cups chopped apples
2 cups cranberries.
Boil all together for 15 minutes, to yield
5 cups juice, when strained. Add
1 pkg. pectin crystals. Bring to the boil.
Add 5-1/2 cups sugar
1/4 cup lemon juice. Boil hard 1 minute.
Bottle, and seal with parowax.

# *Raspberry*

While the native red raspberry is a member of the Rose family, it has various progeny of its own – ranging from the yellow bakeapple, to the salmonberries of the Yukon, the moist dewberry, and British Columbia's cultivated purple loganberry.

Deep summer in Canada is the smell and taste and sight of wild raspberries covering burned-out clearings and edging country lanes. A friend on Cape Breton Island claims that in that paradise the wild raspberries grow as large as Ontario's cultivated fruit. In northern Ontario, the crop is so abundant that another friend retires to her cottage there, each raspberry season, to gather and make the year's supply of jam and jelly. In some rural areas, women and children still add to the family income by selling buckets of wild raspberries to tourists and townspeople.

Raspberry liqueur, raspberry cordial, raspberry wine, have been brewed in Canadian homes each summer since long before Confederation; and perhaps no beverage evokes more nostalgia than old-fashioned raspberry vinegar. When my Aunt Hannah would mix it up for us on a sticky August afternoon, it looked so beautiful in the glass, and felt so sharp and cool in a hot and thirsty child's mouth, that no "soft drink" has ever been able to equal it, in my estimation.

The second edition of *The Thousand Islands Cook Book,* published in Gananoque nearly forty years ago, contains a recipe that is simpler and less time-consuming than most.

## Raspberry Vinegar
[See *Notes* below before proceeding]

Cover wild berries with vinegar and let stand overnight. In the morning, squeeze out the juice. To each pint of juice add a pint of granulated sugar. Boil 10 minutes, then seal in bottles. When serving, add about 3 tsp. to a glass of water. This makes a nice summer drink.

*Notes on the above recipe:*

- I do not "squeeze out" the juice. I drip it thoroughly through a plastic sieve. (Combine with the remaining berries, 2 onions, 1 green pepper, 1 green apple, all chopped fine, 1 tsp. each of salt, cayenne, mace and cinnamon, and 1 cup sugar for each pint of the mixed fruit, and boil gently for 20 minutes. Bottle, and seal with parowax; and when the time for winter feasting arrives, you will serve a chutney that is delicious and different.)
- Two tablespoons makes for a more satisfactory beverage than the suggested 3 teaspoons.
- Soda water, or half soda and half water, produces a really zippy mixture.

## Raspberry Brandy

One need not have access to a hot hearth and a stone jar to try this recipe from the *Canadian Housewife's Manual of Cookery* of 1861. Their modern equivalents produce a satisfying result.

Pick fine dry fruit, put into a stone jar, and the jar into a kettle of water, or on a hot hearth, until the juice will run. Strain, and to every pint add 1/2 lb. of sugar, give one boil, and skim it. When cold, put equal quantities of juice and brandy. Shake and bottle.* Some people prefer it stronger of brandy.†

To each cupful of the berries that are left after straining, add 1/4 cup lemon juice and 1 cup sugar, and boil until it tests for set, for jam.

## Raspberry Conserve

3 qts. raspberries
4 oranges
1 lemon
5 cups sugar
1/4 lb. walnut halves, broken coarsely

Grate the peel of the oranges and lemon into the kettle containing the raspberries. Discard the white layer of each, and add the fruit, diced fine.

At low, then medium heat, bring all to the boil. Add the sugar, and boil for 15 or 20 minutes. Stir in the walnuts, then remove from heat. Let sit for 10 minutes, then bottle, and seal with parowax.

*Salmonberry*

*For beauty's sake, use a clear glass decanter.
†Perhaps some people do – but even as given, this is a beverage of some warmth.

## Raspberry Plum Jelly

2  qts. raspberries
1  qt. ripe red or blue plums

Stone the plums, and add 1/2 cup of water to
them in the preserving kettle. Crushing them all
the while with a wooden spoon or masher, heat
them to boiling. Add the berries, and stir and
crush. Bring all to the boil over medium heat, and
boil gently for 6 or 8 minutes. Strain through a
sieve, then through cloth, to obtain
5  cups juice. Add
1  pkg. pectin crystals.
Bring to the boil, and add 5 cups sugar. Boil hard
for 1 minute. Bottle, and seal with parowax.

### *Other delicious combinations:*

Following the above recipe, try
  Raspberry Rhubarb Jelly
  Raspberry and Gooseberry Jelly
  Raspberry and Saskatoon Jelly
  Raspberry and Red Cherry Jelly
  Raspberry Peach Jelly

## Cardinal Jam

Nearly twenty years ago, the Women's Institute of
Mount Forest, Ontario, published a cookbook of
*Personal Recipes* contributed by their members.
Mrs. Geo. Murphy is to be thanked for this one,
which continues to be a specialty of each rasp-
berry season.

6  cups red raspberries
4  cups pitted sour red cherries
2  cups stemmed red currants
8  cups sugar

Cook until thick – 20 minutes to a half-hour.
Bottle, and seal with parowax.

# Rhubarb

That welcome harbinger of spring, the homely rhubarb, has a long history of medicinal use; but it has also been of prime importance in the art of preserving. Rhubarb is simple to prepare for canning – and, in our day, for freezing. And it combines well with almost any other fruit or vegetable. To name a few, there is rhubarb and saskatoon jam, rhubarb and marrow chutney, rhubarb and strawberry conserve, rhubarb and black currant relish. And there are the exotic "flower jellies" for which rhubarb juice is an excellent base: elderflower jelly, hawthorn bloom jelly, plum blossom jelly.

So many recipes for rhubarb wines are available that it is easy to see why early herbalists labelled it "the wine plant". From the wealth of rhubarb bubbly, wine, shrub, cordial and whiskey recipes, I have selected this tried and true one for

## Rhubarb Champagne

Start this in the early summer, when the rhubarb is full-formed, but juicy and tender.

4 qts. rhubarb, chopped fine
1 gal. cold water
12 young grape-vine leaves, with stems
3-1/2 lbs. sugar
yeast

Crush the chopped rhubarb in a crock with a wooden mallet. Toss in the vine leaves, and over all, half the water, brought to the boil. Cool to lukewarm and add the yeast. Cover and leave in a warm place for 3 days. Strain off the liquor into a fermentation jar, then add the other half of water, which has been brought to a boil with the sugar and cooled to lukewarm. Set it away to work for 5 weeks, then bottle it in strong, champagne-type bottles and wire down the corks. Forget it for at least a year.

## Rhubarb Nectar

Keep a bottle of Rhubarb Nectar in the fridge for cooling drinks throughout the summer.

Boil in 1 qt. water, for 10 minutes,

3 qts. chopped rhubarb
3 oranges, quartered
3 or 4 in. broken cinnamon bark.

Strain thoroughly, so that only the dry pulp is left. Strain the juice through cloth, and boil it for 3 minutes with 1/2 cup sugar for each cup of juice. Cool, and keep in bottles in the refrigerator. Mix half-in-half with soda water or ginger ale, and float an ice cube and a sprig of mint in the top of each glass.

## Rhubarb Marmalade

There are countless recipes for rhubarb conserve and marmalade, with a bewildering variety of combinations – for example, apricots and ginger, orange and banana, red and white currants, figs and lemons. But I always come back to this simple, basic recipe for Rhubarb Marmalade, as given in *Tried and True Recipes,* published in 1911 by the Hospital Auxiliary in Almonte, Ontario. Proceeds from the cookbook helped to furnish rooms, in a day when the advertised cost in the public ward was three dollars and fifty cents a week, and a private room, seven dollars a week.

Peel, core, and grate a large ripe pineapple. Put it in a kettle with 3 times as much tender rhubarb, finely chopped, and 3/4 cup white sugar for each cup of fruit. Let it sit overnight. Next day, boil until the pineapple is clear, then bottle, and seal with parowax.

Sometimes I add the grated peel of a lemon to the marmalade, sometimes a dozen maraschino cherries, or a half-cup of chopped pecans. But it is delicious just as is.

## Rhubarb Mincement

2  cups diced apples
4  cups chopped rhubarb
1  orange, grated peel and juice
1  lemon, grated peel and juice
2  cups brown sugar
1  cup raisins
1  cup currants
1/2  cup citron peel
1/2  cup apple juice or rum
1/2  tsp. each salt, allspice, cloves, nutmeg and cinnamon.

Combine all the ingredients in a large kettle and simmer for 30 minutes. Bottle, and seal with parowax until ready for use in pies.

## Rhubarb Ginger Jelly

3  qts. red rhubarb, chopped
water just to cover

Boil until the rhubarb is soft, then strain through a sieve. Strain the juice through cloth, to measure
5  cups rhubarb juice.
Put in the kettle, with

2  level tsp. ground ginger
1  pkg. pectin crystals.

Bring to the boil, and add

5-1/2  cups sugar.

Boil hard for a full minute. Skim, and bottle. Just before adding the parowax, sprinkle 1/8 tsp. ground ginger on the top of each jar.

# Rose

The Rose family embraces a confusing number of members. To simplify matters, let's consider only roses that are actually called roses.

More specifically, there comes to mind a wide hillside pasture, just off a busy highway, where we wander each June, gathering pails of fragrant wild rose petals. Then, in late autumn, as though not a single bloom had ever been taken, those same bushes are bright with the berries, or hips, that are the fruit of the rose.

While the rose grows wild in areas throughout Canada, it is the flower emblem of the province of Alberta, and there the brilliant hips are sometimes called "Alberta oranges".

Both blossom and fruit are edible; and unusual conserves, syrups and wines have been prepared from them throughout many centuries. Because of the cruel thorns on the branches, the hips are difficult to gather in quantity – but it's worth the trouble, and you can always wear long sleeves and gloves.

First – the bloom. Gather the petals when the sun is on them and they are quite dry. Just close your hand over the rose and pull off all the petals at once, and none of the green. To make syrup or wine, jelly or jam, set to work at once after picking, so that none of the fragrance is lost.

## Rose Petal Wine

2 qts. deep-pink rose petals
1 gal. boiling water
3 lbs. sugar
1/2 cup lemon juice
yeast

Boil together sugar and water and pour it over the petals, in a crock. When it cools to lukewarm, add the yeast, and the lemon juice. Cover with a thick towel, and let it ferment, stirring it with a wooden spoon daily, for 2 weeks. Strain, squeezing every last drop of colour and moisture out of the petals, and set away to work in the fermentation jar. In about 6 weeks, if it is perfectly clear, siphon it off into clear glass bottles and set them away in a cool dark place for at least a year and a half.

## Rose Hip Wine

In earlier days, when imported citrus fruits were luxuries seldom seen on the average table, rose hips were prized for their nutritional value. At present we are in the thick of a rose-hip revival. Health food shops sell dried hips for tea, and as a wine base; and rose-hip syrup is a vitamin C supplement. I was surprised recently, after asking a druggist to recommend some effective eye drops, to discover he had sold me a small bottle of pure rose-hip concentrate!

3 qts. ripe rose hips
1 gal. boiling water
juice of 2 lemons
2-1/2 lbs. sugar
yeast

Put the hips through the food chopper (or blender) and into a crock. Pour the boiling water over them. Cool to lukewarm and add the yeast.

Keep the crock covered, in a warm place, for 8 days, stirring briskly a couple of times each day.

Strain, and add the sugar and lemon juice. Let it work for 4 months in the fermentation jar, before bottling.

## Rose Petal Jelly

Follow the recipe for Rose and Clover Jelly (under Clover), using no clover, and 2 qts. rose petals.

## Rose Hip Jelly

4 qts. ripe rose hips
3 qts. water

Boil together until the hips are soft enough to crush. Strain through cloth, to measure
4 cups rose hip juice. Add

1/2 cup strained lemon juice
1 pkg. pectin crystals.

Bring to the boil, and add

5 cups sugar.

Boil until it tests for set (1 full minute). Bottle, and seal with parowax.

This jelly has a lovely, burnt-orange colour, and a velvety texture.

## Rose Hip and Lemon Jam

Remove the blossom ends from
2 qts. ripe rose hips.
Pour 1 qt. water over them, and boil them until soft. Force through a sieve. To each cup of the puree, allow the grated peel and juice of 1 lemon, and 3/4 cup sugar.
Boil for 10 or 15 minutes – or until it tests for set.

Delicious with hot tea biscuits.

# *Rosemary*

This aromatic herb has small, sharp, stiff leaves, reminiscent of evergreen in both appearance and flavour. It is pungent and spicy. Mix a few leaves of it in sour cream and horseradish, next time you serve baked fish. Tuck a sprig of rosemary beneath each wing of a roasting chicken. And try adding a teaspoon of dried rosemary leaves, next time you make orange marmalade or elderberry jelly. The flavour is anything but elusive, so don't be too lavish with it at first.

## Rosemary Jelly

Bring a cupful of fresh-picked, or 3 tsp. dried rosemary leaves to a full boil in 2 cups water. Cover tightly, remove from heat, and let stand for 15 minutes. Strain through cloth. To 1-1/2 cups of this infusion, add:

    2 cups orange juice, strained
    1/2 cup lemon juice, strained
    1 pkg. pectin crystals.

Bring to the boil, and add

    4 cups sugar.

Boil hard for 1 minute, skim, bottle, and seal with parowax.

Serve it on the tray with cream cheese and biscuits.

# *Rowanberry*

Each October, as I walk along suburban streets, I am saddened by the thought of the innumerable tons of rowanberries that will never see the jelly kettle. The clusters of bright-orange berries look so beautiful in the October afternoon; it is easy to see why the mountain ash, or rowan tree has become a favourite tree for landscaping. But this autumn, before the birds take them all, do experiment with rowanberry wine, jelly, and catsup. The uncooked fruit is very sour, with a sharp, bitter edge to it; but it yields a strong-flavoured jelly, which is excellent with hot roast beef or turkey.

The rowanberry is native to northern Europe, and several European cookbooks offer recipes for Rowanberry Gin and Rowanberry Vodka that sound unquestionably powerful. But we prefer the wine, made with or without a small proportion of apple juice. It is a light, exhilarating wine, lovely to look at as well as to drink.

## Rowanberry Wine

3 qts. ripe rowanberries
1 gal. boiling water
1 qt. apple juice (optional)
3 lbs. sugar
yeast

Wash and stem the berries and pour the boiling water over them in a crock. Let them stand for 10 days, stirring and bruising them daily; then strain off the liquid and add the apple juice, sugar and yeast to it.

Leave the fermentation jar in a warm place for 2 weeks, then set it away to work for 3 or 4 months.

Bottle in strong bottles, with a lump of sugar in each one. Wire down the corks. Store for a year.

## Rowanberry Jelly

4 qts. ripe rowanberries
1 qt. water
1 pkg. pectin crystals
8 cups sugar

Simmer the berries in the water until soft. Mash them. Strain the juice through cloth, to make 7 cups. Bring to the boil and add the sugar. Boil for 1 minute, or until it tests for set.

### *Variation:*

A more mellow jelly is obtained by using half rowanberry juice and half apple juice. If your front lawn flaunts both a flowering crab and a mountain ash, combine the 2 juices. And set a clove in the top of each jar, before you add the parowax.

## Rowanberry Catsup

This old recipe is a spicy, strong-flavoured condiment for cold meats.

2 qts. rowanberries
1 pt. water

Cook until very soft, then force through a sieve [or
use the blender]. To this puree, add:

1 large onion
1 large green pepper
2 large apples,

all chopped very fine. Put in the kettle with:

1 cup vinegar
1 tsp. each of salt, chilli powder, ground cloves
   and allspice
2 cups brown sugar
2 tbsp. honey.

Boil all together, gently, stirring frequently till thick.
(About 20 minutes.) Bottle and seal.

# *Sage*

Shortly after our marriage, we lived for three years on the edge of an out-of-the-way village in northern Saskatchewan. It's long ago; yet sometimes, to this day, the sudden scent of sage will send me back there. Our near neighbours were an elderly Ukrainian couple who lived in a snug sod house with a flourishing garden in front, and a doorway bench where he sat in the summer twilights, playing wild, sad, merry melodies on an accordian. The power line had not yet come through; so there were no street lights to relieve the thick summer darkness. Yet, walking home very late from the village, we always knew when we were exactly abreast of the Ceslack cottage, by the scent of the sage that grew in their herb garden, just inside the fence by the road. It was a sharp, tingling fragrance, stronger than any of the other herbs. Old Mrs. Cesláck gave me my supply each autumn, to dry above the kitchen stove and use in soups and dressings and chicken dumplings, warning me always to use it with a light hand.

Because sage is a ubiquitous perennial, growing wild in many parts of the world, a wealth of folklore has collected throughout the centuries, extolling the plant as a cure-all, a heart's ease, a good luck charm. All sorts of tonic benefits are claimed for sage wine – made in such quantities that one ancient recipe begins, "Boil 25 lbs. Malaga raisins in 26 gallons spring water."

This wine is made on a much more modest scale, but it is very pleasant to drink, especially topped with ice cubes and mint, on a hot summer day.

## Sage Wine

1 pt. young sage leaves
3 lbs. young green rhubarb
1 gal. boiling water
1 lb. raisins or prunes
3 lbs. sugar

Chop fine the rhubarb, sage leaves and raisins (or prunes) and put them in a large bowl or crock. Pour the boiling water over them; cool to lukewarm; and add the yeast. Keep covered, in a warm place, for 14 days, stirring briskly a couple of times each day.

Strain off the liquor; mix the sugar with it, and put all in the fermentation jar to work for a couple of months. Bottle when clear. Store for 1 year.

## Sage and Cider Jelly

Obtain sage infusion by boiling
1 cupful tightly packed, fresh sage leaves or
3 tsp. dried sage.
Boil leaves in 2 cups water for 1 minute. Leave tightly covered, off heat, for 20 minutes.
Strain through cloth, and measure
1-1/2 cups sage infusion. Add
1/2 cup cider vinegar
2 cups pure apple juice
pinch of salt
Bring all to the boil, and add 1 pkg. commercial pectin. Boil hard for 1 minute. Add 2 or 3 drops yellow food colouring and 4 cups sugar. Bottle, and seal with parowax.

Especially good with cheese and crackers, baked fish, or cold sliced turkey.

## Sage Wine Vinegar

2 cups dry white wine
4 cups vinegar
4 whole cloves
1/2 tsp. celery seed
1 tsp. salt
1/2 tsp. fresh-ground pepper

Bring all to the boil and pour it over a pint of fresh-picked sage leaves.

Cover and let stand for a week, stirring and bruising with a wooden spoon, daily. Strain through cloth and set away in tightly corked bottles.

Use it as a base for salad dressings, for basting fish, and as a marinade for beef or lamb.

# Samphire

Having spent most of my life inland, I have never been a gatherer of samphire. But Maritime friends tell me that this low, springy cliff-plant makes delicious pickle. Samphire Pickle is nothing new, either; for the recipe is found in the 1845 edition of *Modern Practical Cookery*.

## To Pickle Samphire

Take the samphire [stems and leaves] when quite green and not too old; lay it in salt and water for 24 hours. Take it out, and simmer it a few minutes in a weak solution of vinegar and water. Drain, and pack in small jars, with some white pepper and ginger in each jar. Boil good vinegar and pour it over to fill up the jars. It will be fit for use in a few days. It is often used for garnishing other pickles, but it is a very good pickle of itself.

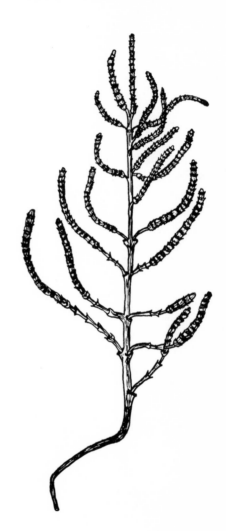

# Saskatoon (Serviceberry)

One of the memorable pleasures of our three years in northern Saskatchewan was the saskatoon berry. They grow there on bushes as low as three feet and as high as young trees; and when they are ripe, in mid-summer, they resemble huckleberries, for they do not have the rich bloom of blueberries. Each summer, we harvested bushels of the fruit, halfway in flavour between an Ontario blueberry and an elderberry. There were fresh saskatoon pies, muffins, steamed puddings, shortcakes; and by mid-August the shelves were filled for winter with saskatoon and rhubarb preserve, spiced saskatoon jelly, saskatoon and apricot jam, and hot saskatoon chutney.

One need not live in Saskatchewan to be able to harvest these juicy, purplish-black berries. They grow wild in all the western provinces and in the Yukon; and a naturalist friend reports finding them in northern Ontario.

## Saskatoon and Apricot Jam

3 qts. ripe saskatoons
1 lb. dried apricots
juice and grated peel of 3 lemons
sugar

Wash the saskatoons and put them in the preserving kettle.

With the scissors, shred the dried apricots into a bowl, and cover them with the grated peel and the juice of the lemons. Cover, and leave overnight. Next day, combine all in the kettle, and heat slowly to a boil. Simmer for 10 minutes. Stir in 3/4 cup sugar for each cup fruit. Boil until it tests for set – about 20 minutes.

# *Strawberry*

Canadian summer begins with strawberries. On that day in mid-June when you come upon the first tiny, ripe wild berry in the short grass of a sunny hillside, you can be sure that in no time at all you'll be knee-deep in daisies and buttercups and devil's paintbrush. Meanwhile, you can fill your mouth with the small, acid fruit, and think about how there is no taste in the world quite like it.

In early Canada, before choice strawberries were widely cultivated, the wild berries must have been eagerly awaited and picked, whether or not one happened to like picking them. The leaves were gathered, too, and brewed into a tea, rich in vitamin C, that was used in the treatment of bowel ailments, sore throat, and liver trouble. Many years ago a country doctor in Ontario devised a strawberry concoction that is sold, to this day, in drug stores as a cure for persistent diarrhea.

A quarter of a century ago, we were newly arrived on Manitoulin Island. On a morning in late June, an Indian woman from the nearby reserve arrived on our doorstep with berries for sale – a pail as large as a scrub-bucket, filled with wild strawberries. The price she asked seemed shamefully small for those hours of picking. Never had I seen so many of them all at once; and for two days the kitchen overflowed with all the things one can do with a bucket of berries: jam, jelly, conserve, and bottles of strawberry syrup to mix with ginger ale and soda water, or to pour over ice cream, come winter. It has never happened again. A cupful or two each season – then we content ourselves with the excellent cultivated varieties.

Strawberries yield a delightful wine; but more often than not its colour has faded, and the full fruit flavour is lacking. Just recently, in the writings of M. A. Jagendorf, an authority on folk wines, I discovered a way of avoiding this, and shall try it next time I make strawberry wine. The recipe that follows owes much to his method.

## Strawberry Wine

4 qts. ripe strawberries, crushed and mashed in a large crock.
1 gal. warm water (not hot)
2 lbs. sugar
yeast

Stir well, then stand the crock, covered, in a warm place for 2 days. Strain, squeezing out of the berries, every last drop of juice. Put the juice in a fermentation vessel, and in about 4 days, when it is fermenting vigorously, add a pint of either gin or vodka. (To quote Jagendorf: "This will set the colour and flavour of the berries, both of which disappear very easily.") Set the jar away to complete fermentation, and when it is completely quiet, bottle it. Strawberry wine matures slowly, and should be forgotten for a full year after the final bottling.

## Strawberry Conserve

There are numerous excellent conserve recipes combining strawberries with rhubarb and orange, figs and bananas, cantaloup and lemon, apple and gooseberry. But our favourite is this one, with just a hint of mint in the flavour.

2 qts. choice ripe strawberries
1 medium-sized ripe pineapple
6 cups sugar
2 tbsp. butter
fresh-picked mint leaves

Grate the pineapple into the kettle (after removing skin and core) and add the washed, stemmed berries. Heat slowly to the boil, meanwhile adding the sugar a cup at a time and stirring gently. Boil for 10 minutes. Add the butter, and boil for 5 minutes more. Bottle, and cool. Place a fresh-picked mint leaf on the top of each jar, and add the parowax.

## Strawberry Preserve I

(An old family recipe that yields a rich, dark, thick preserve.)

In the preserving kettle, mix together:

5 cups sugar
3/4 cup water
2 tbsp. cider vinegar
2 tbsp. butter.

Stir continually as you bring it slowly to the boil, and boil for 5 minutes. Add 6 cups large, firm strawberries, washed, drained, and stemmed. Keep at a boil for 5 minutes. Seal in sterile jars.

## Strawberry Preserve II

(Adapted from *The Canadian Housewife's Manual of Cookery*, 1861.)

In a large bowl, place 3 qts. large, firm, ripe strawberries, and sprinkle as you go with 1-1/2 lbs. white sugar. Leave overnight. Next day, make a syrup by boiling together for 5 minutes:

1 pt. red currant juice (or rhubarb juice)
1-1/2 lbs. sugar

Add to it the contents of the bowl, and simmer until thick, about 10 minutes.

## Strawberry Wine Jelly

2-1/2 cups pure strawberry juice
1 cup dry white wine
1 pkg. pectin crystals
4 cups sugar

Place 3 qts. ripe strawberries in a kettle, over low heat, stirring frequently, until the juice runs freely and you can strain off the required 2-1/2 cups of it. (The berries and any remaining juice can be used for conserve or jam.)

Strain the juice through cloth into the jelly kettle, and add the wine and the pectin. Stir as you bring it to the boil, then add the sugar and boil hard for 1 minute.

# Sumac

There are 2 sumacs – a poisonous, and a non-poisonous. There is no danger of confusing the two. The poison sumac is a swamp bush, bearing its fruit in the form of small, smooth, white berries. The edible one – the Stag Sumac – which covers the hillsides with clumps of crimson beauty every autumn, bears its fruit at the end of each branch, in large cone-shaped clusters of tiny crimson berries matted together to look like thick velvet. The berries have an acid, refreshing taste in sumac-ade; and, being rich in malic acid, like apples, they make a jelly that sets very quickly. Many people today are unaware of this tree's value; but the early settlers made use of it as a beverage, a remedy for skin irritations, and a dye.

To obtain the juice, break off the large red cones, wash them, and just barely cover them with water in the kettle. Boil for 10 minutes, mashing them frequently with a wooden spoon; then strain off all the liquid.

## Sumac Ade

Strain through cloth 3 cups sumac juice [see directions above]. Boil it for 3 minutes, with 2 cups sugar. Keep this syrup in bottles in the refrigerator, and for a cooling drink, add 2 tablespoons of it to a glass of water, or soda water or lemonade.

## Sumac Wine

Follow the directions for Rowanberry Wine, using the apple juice for a wine that is less astringent than pure sumac.

## Sumac and Apple Jelly

2 qts. red sumac heads
1 qt. wild apples

Rinse the sumac heads, and rinse, stem, and remove the blossom end of the wild apples. Cover with water, and boil gently until the apples are soft. Strain all through a sieve, then strain through cloth, to measure 7 cups juice.

Stir in 1 pkg. pectin crystals, and bring to a full boil. Add 8 cups sugar, and boil hard for 1 minute. Bottle, and seal with parowax.

This is a tart jelly. It can be made with all sumac juice, but we prefer the more mellow flavour of sumac mixed with apple.

# *Thyme*

Like so many of the herbs which enliven modern cookery, thyme was grown in the early herb gardens for its medicinal value. Wild Thyme Tea was sipped for many and varied ailments, from flatulence to fever from a cold, and it was prescribed by the herbalists of ancient Rome as a remedy for melancholia. In our day, Euell Gibbons claims that, laced with honey and salt, thyme tea is better than either black coffee or drugs, for the unfortunate sufferer from a hangover.

Thyme is a hardy perennial; if you've planted it in your herb garden, you will be able to pick it all winter, except for those few weeks when it is buried in snow. There are several cultivated varieties; and there is also a wild thyme, which grows in meadows and waste land in many areas of Canada. Use any of them to make this fresh, fragrant jelly, which belongs with fowl, fish or cheese dishes, and with cream cheese and crackers.

## Thyme and Honey Jelly

1 cup fresh-picked thyme leaves
2 cups water.
Cover, and bring to the boil and simmer 1 minute. Remove from heat and leave, covered, for 15 minutes. Strain through cloth.
To 1-3/4 cups of this infusion, add
1/4 cup cider vinegar
2 cups apple juice
1 pkg. pectin crystals,
and bring to the boil.
Stir in 4 cups sugar and a few drops vegetable food colouring, to obtain a shade of green much lighter than mint jelly.
Boil hard for 1 minute, then skim, bottle, and seal with parowax.

# Tomato

September is tomatoes. True, they ripen in August; but by September there is such an abundance of them that everyone with even a dozen plants is forced to do something with the surplus. To this day, as I walk along neighbourhood streets on a September afternoon, I catch myself at the old "counting game" of childhood – by our noses counting the number of houses where chilli sauce was in the making, as we sauntered home after school.

The old name for tomato is "love apple". Edwin C. Guillet, in his *Early Life In Upper Canada* tells us that until about the middle of the nineteenth century, the tomato was considered poisonous, but because they were so colourful and lovely to look at, people hung them up in their houses for decoration. How grateful I am to the unknown, brave individual who made the discovery that he could eat them and live.

A selection of tomato recipes is difficult to make; the wealth of varying chilli sauce recipes, alone, would fill a fat pamphlet. Modern methods of freezing and blending have simplified the process of preserving tomatoes for winter use. If you happen to own dozens of sealers, you may prefer to cling to the canning-them-whole method. Otherwise, this blender recipe uses fewer sealers and allows for a variety of uses. This basic juice – almost a puree – may be used:

- As a tomato cocktail, thinning each serving with 1/3 orange juice, chilled liquid strained from a cooked vegetable, or any dry wine.
- As a base for Italian spaghetti sauce, and a dozen different casserole dishes.
- As a quick and tasty addition to a kettleful of home-made soup.

## Tomato Juice

Put 1/4 cup lemon juice in the blender. Peel tomatoes, and pack them into the blender, bruising them to make their own juice. Add

    2 sticks of celery, broken,
    1 small onion,
    1 tsp. salt and
    1 tsp. worcestershire sauce.

Repeat, as many as the blender will handle each time, until all the tomatoes are used. Pour into containers and freeze at once. Or pour into bottles or sealers and process by the cold-pack canning method.

## Tomato Wine

(An unusual wine, to accompany the meat course, can be made from ripe tomatoes. The recipes vary widely, but all stress the fact that this wine matures slowly and is practically unpalatable unless left for a year. Give it two years.)

Follow the procedure for Parsley Wine, allowing 4 qts. unpeeled ripe tomatoes to 1 gal. water. For a medium dry wine use 3 lbs. of sugar.

## Green Tomato Mince Meat

In 1946, the ladies of Chapter No. 32, Order of the Eastern Star, Elm Creek, Manitoba, published a book of *Star Recipes*. If you wish to have the makings of a mouth-watering mince pie on hand throughout the winter, try this.

3 qts. green tomatoes (chopped fine)

Cover with water and cook slowly 1 hour. Let stand overnight. Drain off water in the morning. Add:

1 qt. chopped apples
1 lb. chopped suet
1 lb. raisins
1/2 lb. currants
1/2 lb. mixed peel
1 cup vinegar
2 lbs. brown sugar

Cook slowly. Just before ready to seal, add 1 tsp. each cinnamon and allspice.

*Note:* You may wish to vary this recipe, contributed to *Star Recipes* by Mrs. Carrie Watchorn – to whom I and several others are grateful. I find mace and coriander to be preferable spices, and favour only half a cup of vinegar (or lemon juice) and the other half cup good rum or brandy.

## Chow Chow

In mid-summer, there are numerous delicacies which can be made from the unripe tomatoes. Small whole spiced pickles, green tomato dills, tomato and apple chutney, and this long-time favourite relish known as Chow Chow. As children, the sound had almost as much appeal as the taste. Even if the dish were right within reach of a small arm, we would chant, "Please pass the chow chow! Please pass the chow chow!"

I have tried several excellent recipes, only to return to this yellowed newspaper clipping in a collection saved and pasted over the printed pages of a Machine Oil booklet by a farmer's wife in Lanark County more than a half-century ago.

Chop fine 4 qts. fresh-picked green tomatoes, and sprinkle them with 1/4 cup salt. Let them stand overnight. Next morning, drain, and add:

1 qt. chopped onion
1 small head cabbage, chopped
3 large red peppers, chopped
2 tsp. dry mustard
1 tsp. tumeric
1 tsp. ground cloves
1 cup brown sugar
1 qt. vinegar

Boil gently for an hour or so, stirring frequently. Bottle and seal.

## Tomato Pineapple Relish

*Home Cooking Secrets* of the Cambridge Street United Church Women of Lindsay, Ontario modernizes an old recipe for Tomato Preserve, under the name of Tomato Pineapple Relish.

2  cups prepared ripe tomatoes
2  tbsp. vinegar
2  tsp. worcestershire sauce
1/2  tsp. ground allspice
6  cups white sugar
1-1/2  cups canned crushed pineapple
1/2  tsp. ground cinnamon
1/4  tsp. ground cloves
1  bottle certo

Scald, peel and chop tomatoes and boil for 10 minutes. Measure 2 cups tomatoes into a large saucepan. Mix with seasonings, pineapple and sugar. Boil hard for 1 minute, stirring constantly. Remove from heat and add certo. Skim off foam. Stir and skim for 5 minutes. Seal with paraffin in sterilized jars.

The earlier recipes for this relish, really a combination of a jam and a relish, do not use certo. But they do add the juice and grated peel of 2 lemons.

## Tomato Wine Jelly

2  cups tomato juice (fresh or canned)
3  tbsp. lemon juice
1/4  tsp. each salt, fresh-ground pepper, and celery seed
1-1/2  cups dry red wine
1  pkg. pectin crystals

Bring these to the boil, and stir in

4  cups sugar.

Boil for 1 minute. Bottle. Set a clove bud in the top of each jar before pouring the parowax.

Serve it with cold roast beef, or spread liberally on bread and butter, with a piece of cheese in the other hand.

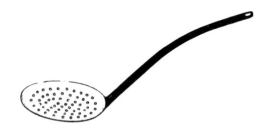

## Spicy Fruit Conserve

An interesting regional cookbook, entitled *From Ottawa Kitchens,* was compiled in 1954, for the benefit of the Canadian Save the Children Fund. Since many of the contributors were wives of foreign ambassadors to Canada, much of the food has an international flavour. There are uncooked chocolate-almond delicacies by Mme. Lyra of the Brazilian Embassy; Carrot Hulwa from Pakistan; Braised Pickled Beef from Germany; and a satisfying supper casserole featuring eggplant, minced beef and cheese, from Mme. Rosetti of the Embassy of Greece. Canadian contributors include the then Chef at the Chateau Laurier Hotel, with his Leek and Potato Soup; Senator Cairine Wilson with Meat Pie; the intrepid Mayor of Ottawa, Charlotte Whitton, with a luscious, calorie-packed dessert appropriately named Charlotte Russe; and this glorified chilli-sauce sort of recipe by Mrs. Nora FitzGerald.

Peel, and cut fine:

5  apples
5  peaches
5  plums
5  pears
5  tomatoes [I use a dozen]
5  cups sugar [I use brown]
3  cups vinegar
1  tbsp. salt
2  tbsp. mixed spices (in a small bag)
*Optional:*
2  tbsp. preserved ginger
2  sticks cinnamon

Cook until thick, about 1 hour. (Remove spice bag.) Put in sterilized jars and seal.

# Wintergreen

In the high, dry woodland, under pines and hard-woods, you will come upon the dark waxen foliage of the wintergreen plant, known by several other names as well – boxberry, spice berry, creeping snowberry, and teaberry. It is a low creeping plant, with shiny, aromatic leaves, some of which turn as red in autumn as the berries they bear. The berries are about the size of a chokecherry, and mealy, with a pungent flavour familiar to everyone who's tasted it in candy, cough syrup, and toothpaste.

Wintergreen Tea and Wine were recommended by pioneer herbalists in the treatment of rheumatism, gout, headache, and lumbago.

## Wintergreen Wine

Gather 2 qts. fresh-picked wintergreen leaves in the fall, and be sure to have some that have turned red, so that your wine will take on a gentle, pink colour.

Pour 1 gal. boiling water over the leaves, in a crock, and let them steep in it for a week. Strain off the liquor, heat it to lukewarm, and add 2 cups honey, 2 cups sugar, and yeast. Set the covered crock in a warm place for 2 weeks; then strain the liquor into a fermentation jar, and let it work away until spring, then bottle it.

This member of the melon, or squash family, is useful both as a vegetable and as a condiment. In season, serve it *sautéd* with tomato and onion, or in a casserole with eggplant and grated cheese. Use it fresh from the vines in late summer for this pickle to accompany winter feasting.

### Zucchini Relish

8 cups chopped zucchini
2 large onions, chopped fine
2 green peppers, chopped fine
1 small hot red pepper, chopped fine
3 green apples, chopped fine
1 cup chopped celery
salt

Prepare zucchini and other vegetables. Sprinkle liberally with salt. Cover and leave overnight. Next day, rinse with cold water and drain thoroughly. Make a sauce of

3 tbsp. flour
2 tbsp. dry mustard
1 tbsp. tumeric
1 tbsp. celery seed
1 tsp. each of alum, salt, and fresh-ground pepper.

Use only enough water to mix these ingredients to a smooth paste. Stir it into 2 cups vinegar brought to the boil with 1 cup sugar, and simmer, stirring continually, until the sauce thickens. Then add the chopped vegetables, and bring all to the boil again, cooking for only 3 minutes.

## Works Cited

Bell, Reverend William, M.A. *Hints to Emigrants.* Edinburgh, Scotland: 1824.

*Blue Magic.* Halifax, N.S.: Nova Scotia Dept. of Agriculture and Marketing.

*Canadian Favourites.* Ottawa: CCF National Council, 1944.

*Canadian Housewife's Manual of Cookery.* Hamilton, Ontario: Printed by Wm. Gillespy, 1861.

*A Centennial Cook Book.* Nurses' Alumnae, Kingston General Hospital, Ottawa Branch, 1967.

*The Cook Not Mad; or Rational Cookery: Being a Collection of Original and Collected Receipts . . .* Kingston, Ontario: Published by J. Macfarlane, 1831.

*Cook Book,* published by the Ladies' Aid of the Christian Church. Newmarket, Ontario: Express-Herald Book and Job Office, 1911.

Fernald, Merritt L. *Edible Wild Plants of Eastern North America.* Rev. ed. New York: Harper and Row, Inc., 1958.

*Fleischman's Recipes.* The Fleischman Co., 1915.

*From Ottawa Kitchens,* recipes from Ottawa hostesses, compiled for the benefit of the Save the Children Fund, 1954.

Garrett, Blanche Pownall. *From the Fruits of the Earth.* Peterborough, Ontario: Centennial Press, 1972.

Gibbons, Euell. *Stalking the Healthful Herbs.* New York: David McKay Co. Inc., 1967.

Graham, W. H. *The Tiger of Canada West.* Toronto: Clarke, Irwin and Co. Ltd., 1962.

Guillet, Edwin C. *Early Life in Upper Canada.* Toronto: Ontario Publishing Co., 1933.

*Home Cooking Secrets of Cambridge Street United Church Women.* Lindsay, Ontario: 1969.

Jagendorf, M.A. *Folk Wines.* New York: Vanguard Press, 1963.

*Letters from Upper Canada.* Published in Dublin, Ireland, 1832.

*Modern Practical Cookery.* Montreal: Armour and Ramsy, 1845.

*New Dominion Monthly,* November 1868 to March 1869, inclusive. Montreal: John Dougall and Son.

*Oxford Book of Food Plants.* Oxford: Oxford University Press, 1969.

*Personal Recipes,* compiled by Mount Forest Women's Institute. Mount Forest, Ontario: 1956.

Pownall, Eva Kirkham. Hand-written cook book kept by my mother. Begun in the early 1900s.

Richardson, E. M. *We Keep a Light.* Revised edition. Toronto: Ryerson Press, 1961.

*Souvenir of Manitoulin Island.* Historical Sketch and Cook Book, 1948.

*Star Recipes.* Published by Elm Creek Chapter, Order of the Eastern Star. Elm Creek, Manitoba: 1946.

*The Thousand Island Cook Book.* 2nd edition. Gananoque, Ontario: 1938.

*363 Home Tested Recipes.* Toronto: Maclean

132

Hunter Pub. Co. Ltd., 1955.

Traill, Catherine Parr. *The Canadian Settler's Guide*. Toronto: The Old Countryman Office, 1855. Also available in New Canadian Library edition. Toronto: McClelland and Stewart Ltd., 1969.

*A Treasury of Newfoundland Dishes*. 5th ed. Sally West, ed., homemaker's consultant, Maple Leaf Milling Co., Newfoundland. Toronto: 1964.

*Tried and True Recipes*. Arranged by the Women's Institute of Almonte, Ontario, 1911.

*The Wimodausis Club Cook Book*. Toronto: Grand and Toy Ltd., 1934.

## Know what you are eating

Brownlow, Margaret. *Herbs and the Fragrant Garden*. 2nd ed. London: Darton, Longman and Todd, 1963.

Canada. Department of Agriculture, Plant Research Institute. *Edible and Poisonous Mushrooms of Canada*. Ottawa, 1962.

Gibbons, Euell. *Stalking the Wild Asparagus*. New York: David McKay Co. Inc., 1962.

Krieger, Louis C. *The Mushroom Handbook*. New York: Dover, 1967.

Montgomery, F. H. *Native Wild Plants of Eastern Canada*. Toronto: McGraw-Hill Ryerson Ltd., 1962.

_____. *Plants from Sea to Sea*. Toronto: The Ryerson Press, 1966.

Peterson, Roger and McKenny, Margaret. *A Field Guide to Wildflowers*. Boston: Houghton Mifflin Co., 1968.

Smith, Alexander. *The Mushroom Hunter's Field Guide*. University of Michigan Press: 1968.

Traill, Catherine Parr. *Canadian Wild Flowers*. Printed and lithographed by Agnes Fitzgibbon, 1968. Facsimile edition published by Coles Pub. Co. Toronto: 1972.

## To read, enjoy and use

Aylett, Mary. *Country Wines.* London: Odhams Press Ltd., 1965.

Benoit, Jehane. *The Art of Mme. Jehane Benoit: Jams, Pickles and Preserves.* Don Mills, Ontario: Pagurian Press, 1972.

Berglund, Berndt and Bolsby, Clare E. *The Edible Wild.* Toronto: Pagurian Press, 1971.

Gaertner, Dr. Erika. *Harvest Without Planting.* Chalk River, Ontario: 1967.

Hume, Rosemary and Downes, Muriel. *Cordon Bleu Book of Jams, Preserves and Pickles.* London: Chatto, 1970.

*Jams, Jellies and Pickles.* Ottawa: Queen's Printer, publication No. 992, 1958.

The Jelly Maker's Manual. Pamphlet published by General Foods Corp., Montreal, 1960.

Kananan Leona, compiled by. *Yukon Cookbook.* Quesnel, B.C.: Big Country Printers Ltd., 1971.

Nightingale, Marie. *Out of Old Nova Scotia Kitchens.* Toronto: Pagurian Press, 1971.

Taylor, (Peggy Frances). *Easy Made Wine and Country Drinks.* Revised ed. London: Elliott, 1959.